The
Environmental
— Sourcebook —

The
Environmental
Sourcebook

EDITH CAROL STEIN

IN COOPERATION WITH THE
Environmental Data Research Institute

Lyons & Burford

PUBLISHERS

Lyons & Burford,
31 West 21 Street,
New York, NY 10010

Printed in the United States of America

10 9 8 7 6 5 4 3 2 1

The author gratefully acknowledges the staff of
the Environmental Data Research Institute, particularly
Dori Hampl, Dora Hanninen, Carl Herrgesell,
Allen Krusenstjerna, and Christine Robbins for their
help in the preparation of this book

LIBRARY OF CONGRESS
CATALOGING-IN-PUBLICATION DATA
Stein, Edith Carol.
The environmental sourcebook / Edith Carol Stein.
p. cm.
Includes bibliographical references and index.
ISBN 1-55821-164-0 (pb)
1. Environmental protection—Abstracts. 2. Environmental
protection—United States—Societies, etc. 3. Human ecology—
Abstracts. 4. Human ecology—United States—Societies, etc.
5. Conservation of natural resources—Abstracts. 6. Conservation of
natural resources—United States—Societies, etc. I. Title.
TD170.S84 1992
363.7—dc20 92-11437
CIP

Contents

Preface

THE PURPOSE OF THIS BOOK IS TO
solve what promises to be a major problem of the 1990s: environmental information overload. Never before has so much information about the environment been available. Every year hundreds of books and articles are written about it. Every day we hear more news about pesticides, beleaguered whales, toxic waste, and climate change. We receive a torrent of mail from environmental groups requesting our time, funds, and support. But it's hard for many of us to make sense of the environmental situation and to find out:

- What are the most urgent issues?
- Which environmental groups work on them?
- What books and periodicals best describe them?
- What foundations fund them?

The Environmental Sourcebook is designed to answer these questions for the concerned citizen seeking orientation to the field. But others already working on environmental issues will also have a use for this book. These include environmental professionals who need information about organizations or publications outside their specialties, activists searching for funding, and donors trying to decide which issues and groups to support.

The goal of this book is to help readers sort out what has become a confusing tangle of information about the environment so they can easily find just what they're looking for.

What's In This Book

THE ENVIRONMENTAL SOURCEBOOK contains twelve chapters: an Overview and chapters on eleven individual issues. Each chapter includes a brief narrative text and resource lists of books, periodicals, organizations, and funding sources. *The Environmental Sourcebook* thus offers both an introduction to environmental issues and a library of resources.

Text and resource lists in the Overview pertain to a broad range of environmental issues. The issues chapters include text synopses and resource lists of books, periodicals, organizations, and funding sources for eleven issues: population, agriculture, energy, climate, biodiversity, water, oceans, solid waste, toxics, endangered lands, and development. Some periodicals or organizations could appear in several chapters, but each is listed just once, under its primary focus. Resources mentioned in the Overview are not relisted in individual chapters.

Entries for periodicals, organizations, and funding sources are standardized as follows:

⊗ Periodicals

Name
Organization/publisher
Address
Telephone and fax
Editor

Type	Magazine, newsletter, or journal
Frequency	How often published
Length	Usual number of pages per issue
Subscription fee	For individuals within the United States. We also indicate when periodicals are available as a membership benefit or when subscription fees for members and nonmembers differ
Topics	Environmental foci
Coverage	Activism, book reviews, business/industry, conference proceedings, education, environmental community, government, law/policy, legislation, litigation, organization activities, research, science
Audience	Intended readership: business/industry, citizens, educators, environmental organizations, government, professional/academic
Geographic scope	Local, state, regional, national, international, or global coverage
References	Yes means sources are documented
Advertising	Yes means the periodical accepts paid advertising from outside sources

Comment

❖ Organizations

Name
Address (main office)
Telephone and fax
CEO/director
Purpose

Founded   Year established
FYR   Fiscal year for financial data reported
Revenue   [Brackets indicate estimate]
Expenditures   [Brackets indicate estimate]
1990 membership
Change from previous year
Staff   Number in main office
Chapters
Affiliates
Topics   Primary environmental foci; for a number
                       of organizations listed in the Overview that
                       work on many topics, only "All environ-
                       mental" is indicated
Approaches   Advocacy, collaboration, conferences, de-
                       monstration projects, direct action, dispute
                       resolution, education, funding, grassroots
                       organizing, land acquisition, legislation,
                       litigation, lobbying, media, policy, publica-
                       tions, research, technical assistance, train-
                       ing, workshops
Scope   Local, state, regional, national, interna-
                       tional, or global
Special projects   Campaigns or programs for 1991 to 1992
Periodicals   Magazines, newsletters, or journals pub-
                       lished
Books   Yes means the organization publishes books
Reports   Yes means the organization publishes re-
                       ports

❑ Foundation Funding

This category will be of interest to those individuals or groups already working in the field. Funding for conservation and environmental purposes has historically been a small part of overall philanthropic giving in this country. For the 35,000 or so independent and community foundations, environmental funding in 1990 accounted for about 5 percent of all dollars awarded.

The lists of funders at the end of the Overview and issues

chapters are drawn from a database of more than 10,000 grants awarded for environmental purposes since 1988 by several hundred U.S. independent and community foundations. Ten of the top funders for each issue (except population) are listed, along with numbers of grants and total dollars awarded in calendar year 1990.

The database is compiled and maintained by Environmental Data Research Institute (EDRI), a nonprofit organization that provides information on funding to the environmental community. With the exception of "population" (which EDRI does not track), the eleven issues outlined in *The Environmental Sourcebook* correspond to fields in the EDRI database.

1

Overview

WITHIN THE LAST DECADE OR TWO, the environment has gradually shifted from the domain of special-interest groups to the center of public concern. The trend accelerated in the late 1980s as media reports on such topics as medical waste, rain forest destruction, oil spills, and climate change galvanized public opinion. The response was dramatic: Huge numbers of citizens joined environmental efforts of one sort or another. Established organizations grew and new ones were formed.

The environment has become a growth industry unto itself. According to the Internal Revenue Service, upwards of 12,000 nonprofit organizations now work in conservation or related areas. There are now "green" companies and products and even "green" investment firms.

Some social scientists think the environmental movement represents a profound social change: first, because the environmental movement is so extraordinarily broad based, with ample room for radical activists such as Earth First! and Sea

Shepherd as well as the more traditional groups; and second, because it challenges the dominant Western worldview and its three assumptions:

- Unlimited economic growth is possible and beneficial.
- Most serious problems can be solved by technology.
- Environmental and social problems can be mitigated by a market economy with some state intervention.

Since the 1970s, we've heard increasingly about the competing paradigm, wherein:

- Growth must be limited.
- Science and technology must be restrained.
- Nature has finite resources and a delicate balance that humans must observe.

During the publicized excesses of the 1980s, these points were often ignored. But it's now the 1990s and we're again hearing catchphrases about "limits to growth," "small is beautiful," and "making do with less." These things haven't really happened yet: We're talking a lot about recycling, energy conservation, and preservation of the Earth, but most of us have yet to change our ways and do without.

Still, there's an enormous amount of activity on the environmental front. Like any other deeply rooted social movement, the environmental movement has its own momentum —its fashions, buzzwords, and fads. Just now, for instance, it's fashionable to talk of NGOs (nongovernmental organizations), North-South communication (between the developed and the developing countries), minority participation, and sustainable development.

Resource lists at the end of the Overview and each of the subsequent issues chapters—while not comprehensive—should give the reader a taste of the enormous variety of noteworthy publications and organizations available, as well as a sense of just how much is going on.

RESOURCES

Just a few years ago, there was simply nowhere to turn for an overview of environmental issues or an organized list of things to do to save the world. Today, still basking in the afterglow of Earth Day 1990, we find almost too many choices. The books vary widely in approach and quality. We describe some of the best ones here.

☞ Books and Reports

Blueprint for the Environment: A Plan for Federal Action. T. Allan Comp, editor. Salt Lake City: Howe Brothers. 1988, 300 pp.

Written by a coalition of seventeen environmental organizations in November 1988 as advice to then President-elect Bush, *Blueprint* addresses thirteen major environmental problems and suggests means for their remedy. The central theme: The United States, one of the wealthiest and most powerful of nations, must take a leadership role in solving international environmental problems. Now joined by so many other books in a rapidly evolving field, this book is perhaps most interesting for its perspective on what "the environmental president" might have done.

Design for a Livable Planet: How You Can Help Clean Up the Environment. Jon Naar. With a foreword by Frederic D. Krupp. New York: Harper & Row Publishers. 1990, 338 pp.

One of the better 1990 Earth Day books, this one examines nine issues: air quality, acid rain, deforestation, energy, garbage, global warming, radiation, toxics, and water. It also has chapters on environmental law, eco-action, and green consumerism. *Design* is proactivist, but every chapter offers of a lot of solid data, followed by a page or two on what you can do, and extensive resource lists. Its major flaws are its sometimes confusing format and dull graphics.

The Earth Care Annual 1991. Russell Wild, editor. With a foreword by Jay D. Hair and an introduction by Robert Rodale. Emmaus, PA: Rodale Press. 1990, 236 pp.

This book has sections on ten issues: garbage, global warming, oceans, ozone, pesticides, polar regions, toxic waste, tropical forests, waterways, and wildlife. There is an additional section on Earth Day. Each section contains three to seven articles written in 1990 by various authors and originally published in several newspapers and magazines. The articles document environmental success stories from a Maine fisherman's efforts to ban ocean dumping to a German-born herpetologist's studies of tropical forest iguanas.

Earth Right. H. Patricia Hynes. Rocklin, CA: Prima Publishing & Communications. 1990, 236 pp.

This book reviews global warming, ozone, solid waste, toxics, and water. Each issue is described in three to five short chapters. The last exhorts the citizen to action and is followed by a brief resource list. Earth Right's strident tone and mix of personal anecdotes and facts undercut its appeal.

Ecologue: The Environmental Catalogue and Consumer's Guide for a Safe Earth. Bruce N. Anderson, editor. New York: Prentice Hall Press. 1990, 255 pp.

This book addresses the lifestyle changes needed to mitigate environmental problems (from energy to waste). Organized by product use (baby care, education/fun) or type of commodity (appliances) rather than environmental issues, *Ecologue* deals with principles (how to conserve energy) rather than just what to buy. Perhaps the main problem with this type of book is that it teaches us how to consume (again) when the real issue is how not to consume at all.

50 Simple Things Kids Can Do To Save the Earth. The EarthWorks Group. Kansas City, MO: Andrews & McMeel. 1990, 156 pp.

Younger sibling to the original *50 Things You Can Do*, this book suggests practical things children—and their parents—can do.

50 Things You Can Do To Save the Earth. The EarthWorks Group. Berkeley, CA: Earthworks Press. 1989, 96 pp.

The runaway best-seller of Earth Day 1990, this book is neat, simple, and to the point. Not to be missed (but don't expect anything very thought-provoking either).

Gaia: An Atlas of Planet Management. Norman Myers, general editor. With a foreword by Gerald Durrell. New York: Anchor Press, Doubleday. 1984, 272 pp.

No ordinary atlas, this one is packed with facts and illustrated with wonderful drawings and pictographs. The "Gaia" of the title refers to the hypothesis that the biosphere, atmosphere, oceans and soil form a self-regulating system maintaining optimal conditions for life on Earth. But this book does not substitute philosophy for fact: Its text and pictures contain a huge amount of information. A persuasive introduction to world ecology for lay readers of all ages.

The Global Citizen. Donella H. Meadows. Washington, DC: Island Press. 1991, 300 pp.

A collection of pieces on the environment by the principal author of *The Limits to Growth.* These originally appeared in a syndicated newspaper column, "The Global Citizen," and include such topics as "The Thinning of Turnips and the Right to Life" and "Incinerator Blues: Do You Know Where Your Garbage Is Tonight?"

The Global Ecology Handbook: What You Can Do About the Environmental Crisis. The Global Tomorrow Coalition. Walter H. Corson, editor. Boston, MA: Beacon Press. 1990, 414 pp.

This guide to environmental issues and action is easily the best of the many books of this type released amidst the 1990 Earth Day frenzy. *Handbook,* the handiwork of the Global Tomorrow Coalition, a collaborative group of 115 environmental organizations, was designed as companion guide to the 1990 PBS series *Race to Save the Planet.* Go to this book for a sound introduction to major issues and strategies for action as well as generous lists of books, films, and teaching aids.

The Green Consumer. John Elkington, Julia Hailes, and Joel Makower. New York: Penguin Books, Tilden Press. 1990, 342 pp.

One of the best guides for the environmentally conscious consumer, *Consumer* explains the impact of everyday choices and provides data on companies and products. Readings grouped by issue and an alphabetical list of major organizations are included.

The Green Pages. The Bennett Information Group. New York: Random House. 1990, 235 pp.

A sort of *Consumer Reports* on products and their environmental impact, *Pages* is similar to *Ecologue,* but better organized. It consists of three parts: the market shopper's guide, the mail-order shopper's guide, and a guide to environmental issues. Parts one and two are each divided according to living spaces: the laundry, the kitchen, etc. This book lists over 900 individual products and their environmental characteristics. What this book does not do is give a *Consumer Reports* type of product assessment: a comparison of efficacy or price. The introduction and part three both outline environmental issues (from acid rain to waste). These sections are brief and germane. A useful little book, small enough to be carried to market.

The 1992 Information Please Environmental Almanac. Compiled by World Resources Institute. Boston, MA: Houghton Mifflin Company. 1992, 606 pp.

As would be expected, this almanac provides facts and figures, charts and graphs. It has chapters on nine environmental issues as well as profiles of individual countries, states, and U.S. cities. It includes a historical timeline and an assessment of the planet's health in 1991. This book provides the background data that other sources often omit. Its major flaw is its negative focus: It gives a lot of information on the problems, but little about what has been done to remedy them.

One Earth, One Future: Our Changing Global Environment. National Academy of Sciences. Washington, DC: National Academy Press. 1990, 195 pp.

Derived from a National Academy of Sciences conference, this book attempts to put current environmental events into the perspective of geologic time. It describes interactions among the atmosphere, oceans, land, and water as well as the special issues of population, agriculture and industry. Then it looks in some depth at climate change: global warming, ozone depletion and acid rain and their effects on soils, coasts, and forests. *One Earth* contains just enough science to stimulate thought without overwhelming the casual reader.

Our Common Future. The World Commission on Environment and Development. New York: Oxford University Press. 1988, 400 pp.

The World Commission on Environment and Development, headed by Norwegian Prime Minister Gro Harlem Brundtland, was set up by the United Nations in 1983. Its mission: to propose environmental strategies for achieving sustainable development by the year 2000; to recommend means of greater cooperation among developing countries; and to consider how the international community might better cope with environmental concerns.

Chapters discuss sustainable development, the role of the international economy, population, food, endangered species, energy, industry, cities, the commons, and peace. *Future* proceeds from the optimistic premise "that people can build a future that is more prosperous, more just and more secure." But most of the data presented suggest that the likelihood of such a future is dim indeed.

Saving the Earth: A Citizen's Guide to Environmental Action. Will Steger and Jon Bowermaster. New York: Alfred A. Knopf. 1990, 306 pp.

This somber and rather disappointing large-format book covers eleven environmental problems—their causes, effects, and solutions. Suggestions for individual and government action, further reading, and organizations to contact follow the text for each issue. Although it contains a lot of facts and figures, *Saving* is often anecdotal and fails to convince.

State of the Ark: An Atlas of Conservation in Action. Lee Durrell. With a foreword by Gerald Durrell. New York: Doubleday. 1986, 224 pp.

The ark is the theme for this beautiful and compelling large-format book on endangered species and biodiversity. Color photographs and drawings enhance the text, itself a nice balance between principles of ecology and case studies of successful species-preservation projects.

The State of the Earth Atlas. Joni Seager, editor. New York: Simon & Schuster. 1990, 127 pp.

Not as beautiful as *Gaia*—nor nearly as accessible—this little book contains a lot of information displayed in colorful international maps. At a glance, the reader can identify the environmental hot spots: where population is densest, tropical rain forests most ravaged, cities with the worst air quality, agriculture that is most dependent on chemical fertilizers, etc. Each map is described concisely at the end of the book. Well worth a look, this could be a great classroom tool.

State of the World, 1991. Lester R. Brown et al. Worldwatch Institute. New York: W. W. Norton & Company. 1992, 250 pp.

The Worldwatch Institute is widely recognized as a central source for comprehensive, reliable information about the current state of the environment. *State* is its annual volume, a compendium of shorter issue briefs published throughout each year. Its thoughtful discussions make this book required reading for the environmentally concerned novice and professional.

United Nations Environment Programme: Environmental Data Report. Prepared for the United Nations Environment Programme (UNEP) by the Monitoring and Assessment Research Centre, London, U.K., in cooperation with World Resources Institute, International Institute for Environment and Development, and the U.K. Department of the Environment, London. New York: Basil Blackwell. 1989, 57 pp.

Lots of data here, but this volume is much less attractive and accessible to the general reader than many others in this list.

Whole Earth Ecolog: The Best of Environmental Tools and Ideas.
New York: Harmony Books. 1990, 128 pp.

A special issue in the *Whole Earth Catalog* series, published annually since 1968. This guide to environmental tools has something to say about everything environmental: from the sublime (bicycles and solar energy) to the mundane (water-saving toilets and energy-efficient light bulbs). A great source for the names and addresses that can help you do, learn, and shop for the environment.

World Resources 1990–91. World Resources Institute. New York: Oxford University Press. 1990, 383 pp.

A biannual publication from the World Resources Institute, this book has become *the* authoritative source for the serious student of the environment. Mostly text, this large-format book presents clear summaries and some detailed data supplemented with citations, tables, charts, and maps. Each edition has special foci: This one examines global warming and Latin America in particular detail.

✪ Periodicals

Ambio
Pergamon Press, Inc.
Fairview Park
Elmsford, NY 10523
Phone: 914-592-7700   Fax: 914-592-3625
Elizabeth Kessler, Editor-in-Chief
Type: Journal
Frequency: 8 issues per year
Length: 50 pp.
Subscription fee: $61
Topics: All environmental, but especially atmospheric deposition, forest decline, groundwater, marine issues
Coverage: Policy, research
Audience: Citizens, professional/academic
Scope: International

References: Yes
Comment: A superb scientific journal from Sweden that documents global issues such as acid deposition and climate change with elegance and scientific rigor.

The Amicus Journal
Natural Resources Defense Council
40 West 20th Street, 11th Floor
New York, NY 10011
Phone: 212-727-2700   Fax: 212-727-1773
Francesca Lyman, Editor
Type: Journal
Frequency: Quarterly
Length: 70 pp.
Subscription fee: $10; free to members
Topics: All environmental
Coverage: Book reviews, business/industry, environmental community, government, legislation, litigation, organization activities, policy
Audience: Citizens, environmental organizations
Scope: International
Comment: Informative and always worth reading, with in-depth coverage of a broad range of environmental issues. Regularly includes poetry.

Audubon
National Audubon Society
950 Third Avenue
New York, NY 10022
Phone: 212-832-3200   Fax: 212-593-6254
Mike Robbins, Editor
Type: Magazine
Frequency: Bimonthly
Length: 150 pp.
Subscription fee: $20
Topics: All environmental
Coverage: Activism, legislation, organization activities, policy, research
Audience: Citizens

Scope: National
Advertising: Yes
Comment: Now with a new editor, this impressive glossy contains articles on the full range of environmental issues, great photography, and even enticing ads.

Audubon Activist

National Audubon Society
950 Third Avenue
New York, NY 10022
Phone: 212-546-9100
Fred Baumgarten, Editor
Type: Newsletter
Frequency: Monthly except July and August
Length: 8 pp.
Subscription fee: $20; free to members on request
Topics: All environmental
Coverage: Activism, environmental community, legislation, policy
Audience: Citizens
Scope: National
Comments: An extremely useful guide for activists, with concise, thoughtful articles and updates on the status of legislation. Detailed information on what you can do, where to write, and where to call helps readers act on their beliefs.

Buzzworm

Buzzworm, Inc.
1818 16th Street
Boulder, CO 80302
Phone: 303-442-1969   Fax: 303-442-4875
Joseph E. Daniel, Editor
Type: Magazine
Frequency: Bimonthly
Length: 100 pp.
Subscription fee: $18
Topics: All environmental, but especially conservation and natural resources
Coverage: Activism, environmental community, organization activities, research

Audience: Citizens, environmental organizations
Scope: International
Advertising: Yes
Comment: A lively new magazine filled with reports and photo-essays about topics from the Nepal fur trade to environmental green products and adventure travel outfitters. Specialized directories of organizations, zoos, ecotours, and the like are especially useful.

C.L.F.

Conservation Law Foundation of New England
3 Joy Street
Boston, MA 02108
Phone: 617-742-2540   Fax: 617-523-8019
Daniel Grossman, Editor
Type: Newsletter
Frequency: Quarterly
Length: 8 pp.
Subscription fee: $30
Topics: All environmental, but especially coastal issues, energy efficiency, environmental law, public health, resources management, utilities, water pollution and use, wilderness
Coverage: Activism, business/industry, organization activities, policy
Audience: Citizens, environmental organizations
Scope: Regional (New England)
Comment: Describes some of CLF's efforts to defend the natural resource base of New England.

E Magazine

Earth Action Network, Inc.
28 Knight Street
Norwalk, CT 06851
Phone: 203-854-5559   Fax: 203-866-0602
Doug Moss, Editor
Type: Magazine
Frequency: Bimonthly
Length: 70 pp.
Subscription fee: $20
Topics: All environmental

Coverage: Activism, book reviews, environmental community, organization activities
Audience: Citizens
Scope: National
Advertising: Yes
Comment: This new magazine covers the environmental globescope from an activist perspective. Like *Buzzworm,* but unlike *Audubon* and *Sierra,* this publication is not tied to the agenda of a specific environmental group.

Earth Island Journal
Earth Island Institute
300 Broadway, Suite 28
San Francisco, CA 94133
Phone: 415-788-3666   Fax: 415-788-7324
Gar Smith, Editor
Type: Journal
Frequency: Quarterly
Length: 46 pp.
Subscription fee: $25
Topics: All environmental
Coverage: Activism, environmental community, organization activities, research
Audience: Citizens, educators, environmental organizations
Scope: International
Advertising: Yes
Comment: A powerful journal with eco-activist newsbriefs from all over the world, sometimes about Earth Island Institute-supported activities such as the dolphin-tuna agreement signed in 1990.

Ecological Economics
Elsevier Science Publishing Co., Inc.
655 Avenue of the Americas
New York, NY 10010
Phone: 212-989-5800   Fax: 212-663-3990
Judy Stone, Editor
Type: Journal
Frequency: Quarterly
Length: 100 pp.

Subscription fee: $238
Topics: All environmental, but especially conservation projects, development, ecological economics, sustainable economic development
Coverage: Book reviews, organization activities, research
Audience: Professional/academic
Scope: International
References: Yes
Advertising: Yes
Comment: Scholarly pieces present views from proponents of this new discipline that describes how to account for environmental costs. Some are quite technical, others accessible to the lay reader. A recent example: "Carrying Capacity as a Tool of Development Policy: The Ecuadoran Amazon and the Paraguayan Chaco."

Environment
Heldref Publications
1319 18th Street, NW
Washington, DC 20036-1802
Phone: 202-296-6267   Fax: 202-296-5149
Barbara T. Richman, Managing Editor
Type: Journal
Frequency: 10 issues per year
Length: 50 pp.
Subscription fee: $48
Topics: All environmental
Coverage: Book reviews, organization activities, research
Audience: Citizens, professional/academic
Scope: International
References: Yes
Comment: A fine scholarly journal that often reports on policy issues. Recent articles: "Coastal Erosion and Our Retreat from the Tide," "Obstacles and Opportunities for a Consumer Ecolabel," "Waste Management—Biological Treatment of Hazardous Wastes."

Environment Reporter
Bureau of National Affairs, Inc.
9435 E. West Avenue

Rockville, MD 20850
Phone: 800-372-1033   Fax: 800-253-0332
Sal Bowman, Editor
Type: Newsletter
Frequency: Weekly
Length: 46 pp.
Subscription fee: $2,079 ($1,734 for renewal)
Topics: All environmental
Coverage: Business/industry, legislation, policy, research
Audience: Business/industry, citizens, environmental organizations, professional/academic
Scope: National
Comment: Perhaps the single most valuable periodical for keeping up with environmental events and policy.

Environmental Action
Environmental Action, Inc.
1525 New Hampshire Avenue, NW
Washington, DC 20036
Phone: 202-745-4870   Fax: 202-745-4880
Rose Marie L. Audette and Hawley Truax, Co-Editors
Type: Newsletter
Frequency: Bimonthly
Length: 30 pp.
Subscription fee: $20
Topics: All environmental, but especially air pollution, hazardous waste, minorities, population, radioactive waste, solid waste, Superfund
Coverage: Activism, environmental community, organization activities, research
Audience: Citizens
Scope: International
Advertising: Yes
Comment: The activist's view of the issues.

Environmental Ethics
University of North Texas
Department of Philosophy
P.O. Box 13496
Denton, TX 76203-3496

Phone: 817-565-2727   Fax: 817-565-4448
Eugene C. Hargrove, Editor-in-Chief
Type: Journal
Frequency: Quarterly
Length: 100 pp.
Subscription fee: $18
Topics: All environmental, but especially conservation, ecological ethics, wilderness, wildlife management
Coverage: Book reviews, organization activities, policy
Audience: Citizens, professional/academic
Scope: Global
References: Yes
Comment: A wonderfully interesting journal that discusses philosophical aspects of environmental problems. Examples: "Means and Ends in Wildlife Management," "How Deep Is Deep Ecology?"

EPA Journal
United States Environmental Protection Agency
Superintendent of Documents
Government Printing Office
Washington, DC 20402
Phone: 202-783-3238
John Heritage, Editor
Type: Newsletter
Frequency: Bimonthly
Length: 60 pp.
Subscription fee: $8
Topics: All environmental
Coverage: Legislation, organization activities, research
Audience: Citizens, environmental organizations
Scope: National
Comment: At $8, a subscription to this publication is a bargain. Articles within an issue generally focus on a single topic such as water or waste.

Future Survey
World Future Society
4916 St. Elmo Avenue
Bethesda, MD 20814–6089

Phone: 301-656-8274
Michael Marien, Editor
Type: Newsletter
Frequency: Monthly
Length: 16 pp.
Subscription fee: $75
Topics: All environmental, population
Coverage: Policy, publications, research
Audience: Business/industry, citizens, environmental
    organizations, government, professionals
Scope: International
Comment: A monthly review of the current literature—recent
    books and articles on a wide range of environmental topics
    including national and global trends, forecasts, and policy
    alternatives.

High Country News

High Country Foundation
Grand Avenue
P.O. Box 1090
Paonia, CO 81428
Phone: 303-527-4898
Lawrence Mosher, Editor
Type: Newsletter
Frequency: Biweekly; monthly in January and July
Length: 20 pp.
Subscription fee: $24
Topics: All environmental, but especially forests, mining, natu-
    ral resources, rangelands, water use, wilderness
Coverage: Activism, environmental community, organization
    activities
Audience: Citizens
Scope: Regional
Advertising: Yes
Comment: One of the best sources for news and happenings
    about natural resource issues in the West.

International Environmental Affairs

University Press of New England
17 1/2 Lebanon Street

Hanover, NH 03755
Phone: 603-646-3349   Fax: 603-643-1540
Konrad von Moltke, Editor
Type: Journal
Frequency: Quarterly
Length: 100 pp.
Subscription fee: $45
Topics: All environmental, but especially conservation projects, international lending institutions, sustainable economic development
Coverage: Book reviews, organization activities, research
Audience: Professional/academic
Scope: International
Comment: An excellent journal with substantive scholarly pieces often on key global issues such as climate change or sustainable development.

Orion Nature Quarterly
Myrin Institute, Inc.
136 East 64th Street
New York, NY 10021
Phone: 212-758-6475   Fax: 212-748-6784
George K. Russell, Editor-in-Chief
Type: Magazine
Frequency: Quarterly
Length: 70 pp.
Subscription fee: $14
Topics: All environmental
Coverage: Book reviews, organization activities, research
Audience: Citizens
Scope: International
Comment: Perhaps the most elegant of the glossy environmental magazines, *Orion* is in some ways also the most intriguing. It is published in association with Conservation International.

Our Planet
United Nations Environment Programme (U.S.)
2 United Nations Plaza, Room 803
New York, NY 10017

Phone: 212-963-8139   Fax: 212-963-7341
Shane Cave, Editor
Type: Newsletter
Frequency: Bimonthly
Length: 20 pp.
Subscription fee: Free
Topics: All environmental
Coverage: Book reviews, organization activities, research
Audience: Citizens, environmental organizations, government, professional/academic
Scope: International
Comment: Well-written short pieces on critical issues of environmental science and policy published by the Nairobi-based United Nations Environment Programme.

Resources

Resources for the Future
1616 P Street, NW
Washington, DC 20036
Phone: 202-328-5000   Fax: 202-265-8069
Samuel Allen, Managing Editor
Type: Newsletter
Frequency: Quarterly
Length: 20 pp.
Subscription fee: Free
Topics: All environmental, but especially economic analysis, policy
Coverage: Organization activities, research
Audience: Citizens, environmental organizations
Scope: International
Comment: Reports on research and policy analysis covering the range of environmental issues, written by academicians and RFF scholars. A recent issue targeted global warming: the cost and economic incentives for carbon dioxide abatement and strategies for adaptation to climate change.

Sierra

Sierra Club Foundation
730 Polk Street
San Francisco, CA 94109

Phone: 415-923-5679   Fax: 415-776-0350
Jonathan F. King, Editor-in-Chief
Type: Magazine
Frequency: Bimonthly
Length: 140 pp.
Subscription fee: Free to members
Topics: All environmental
Coverage: Book reviews, environmental community, organization activities, policy, research
Audience: Citizens
Scope: International
Advertising: Yes
Comment: Recently focusing more on coverage of environmental controversies and hot spots, *Sierra* also includes nature writing, biography, articles for kids, and notes on Sierra Club outings. Indisputably one of the most important of the mainstream environmental magazines.

Worldwatch

Worldwatch Institute
1776 Massachusetts Avenue, NW
Washington, DC 20036
Phone: 202-452-1999   Fax: 202-296-7365
Lester R. Brown, Editor
Type: Magazine
Frequency: Bimonthly
Length: 40 pp.
Subscription fee: $15
Topics: All environmental
Coverage: Book reviews, environmental community, law/policy, research
Audience: Citizens, educators, environmental organizations
Scope: International
Comment: This fine publication has short, well-researched articles with a similar flavor to the more lengthy ones in the Worldwatch Paper series.

❖ Organizations

Center for Policy Alternatives
1875 Connecticut Avenue, NW, Suite 710
Washington, DC 20009
Phone: 202-387-6030   Fax: 202-986-2539
Linda Tarr-Whelan, President and Executive Director
Purpose: To promote progressive policy for state and local government on a variety of issues. Current focus is on public capital, democratic participation, economic development, the environment, family and work, sustainable agriculture, and women's economic justice.
Founded: 1975
FYR: 1990
Revenue: $1,205,811
Expenditures: $1,121,175
Staff: 25
Topics: Energy, reproductive freedom, social justice, sustainable development, women
Approaches: Conferences, education, grassroots organizing, policy, publications, research
Scope: State
Periodicals: *Ways and Means* (newsletter)

Center for Resource Economics
1718 Connecticut Avenue, NW, Suite 300
Washington, DC 20009
Phone: 202-232-7933   Fax: 202-234-1328
Charles C. Savitt, President
Purpose: To perform policy studies and research for Island Press, the nonprofit environmental publishing house.
Founded: 1978
FYR: 1990
Revenue: Not available
Expenditures: Not available
Staff: 4
Affiliates: Island Press
Topics: All environmental
Approaches: Policy, research
Scope: International

Conservation Law Foundation of New England
3 Joy Street
Boston, MA 02108-1497
Phone: 617-742-2540   Fax: 617-523-8019
Douglas I. Foy, Executive Director
Purpose: A public-interest law group that promotes efficient resource management, environmental protection, and public health in New England.
Founded: 1966
FYR: 1990
Revenue: [$1,800,000]
Expenditures: [$1,600,000]
1990 membership: 5,000
Staff: 30
Chapters: 2
Topics: Agricultural land preservation, coastal issues, forests, land conservation, least-cost approach, natural resources, solid waste incineration and source reduction, utilities, water use
Approaches: Advocacy, education, litigation, lobbying, policy, research
Scope: Regional (New England)
Special projects: Suit against the Environmental Protection Agency for failure to ensure federal hazardous waste cleanup; encouraging utilities to invest in energy conservation
Periodicals: *CLF* (newsletter)
Books: Yes

Co-op America
2100 M Street, NW, Suite 403
Washington, DC 20063
Phone: 202-872-5307   Fax: 202-223-5821
Alisa Grovitz, Executive Director
Purpose: With the goal of economic sustainability, this group educates consumers and businesses with *Shopping for a Better World* and other publications describing how to align buying and investing habits with values of peace, cooperation, and environmental protection.
Founded: 1981

FYR: 1990
Revenue: $2,000,000
Expenditures: $2,000,000
1990 membership: 52,000
Change from 1989: +15%
Staff: 24
Topics: All environmental, but especially accountability, consumers, environmental protection, environmental sustainability
Approaches: Direct action, education, grassroots organizing, publications, research
Scope: National
Special projects: Valdez Principles; Circle of Poison Prevention Act, 1992; Recover the Earth Rainforest Program
Periodicals: *Co-op America Quarterly* (magazine)

Earth Island Institute
300 Broadway, Suite 28
San Francisco, CA 94133
Phone: 415-788-3666   Fax: 415-788-7324
John Knox and David Phillips, Co-Executive Directors
Purpose: To facilitate broad, interdisciplinary environmental projects as it works to include a greater variety of people in the environmental movement.
Founded: 1986
FYR: 1989
Revenue: $1,164,000
Expenditures: $1,117,000
1990 membership: 35,000
Change from 1989: +10%
Staff: 20
Topics: All environmental, but especially marine issues, minorities
Approaches: Advocacy, conferences, education, funding, grassroots organizing, litigation, policy, publications
Scope: International
Special projects: Urban Habitat Program, Save the Dolphins
Periodicals: *Earth Island Journal* (journal)

Earthwatch
680 Mount Auburn Street
P.O. Box 403
Watertown, MA 02272
Phone: 617-926-8200   Fax: 617-926-8532
Brian A. Rosborough, President
Purpose: Earthwatch offers the citizen a chance to join expeditions engaged in ecologic research. The range of expeditions is enormous—from Sonoran calderas (the mechanism of a volcano's collapse) to Bohemian forests (the effects of acid rain) to the rain forests of Costa Rica (the invasion of exotic plants).
Founded: 1971
FYR: 1990
Revenue: Not available
Expenditures: Not available
1990 membership: 72,000
Staff: 70
Chapters: 3
Topics: All environmental, but especially environmental tourism, research expeditions
Approaches: Direct action, education, publications, research
Scope: International
Periodicals: *Earthwatch* (magazine), *Earth Corps* (newsletter)
Reports: Yes

Environmental Action, Inc.
1525 New Hampshire Avenue, NW
Washington, DC 20036
Phone: 202-745-8470   Fax: 202-745-4880
Ruth Caplan, Director
Founded: 1970
FYR: 1990
Revenue: $407,455
Expenditures: $468,908
1990 membership: 20,000
Staff: 30
Purpose: Building a grassroots movement to demand public accountability for a host of environmental issues.

Topics: All environmental, but especially accountability, air pollution, energy efficiency, hazardous substances, minorities, radioactive waste, right to know, transportation policy

Approaches: Advocacy, direct action, grassroots organizing, lobbying, policy, publications

Scope: National

Special projects: Dirty Dozen Campaign (environmentalists' twelve greatest foes in Congress); Clean Motion Campaign; Toxics Education, Action, and Mobilization Campaign

Periodicals: *Environmental Action* (magazine), *Power Line* (newsletter), *Wastelines* (newsletter)

Books: Yes

Environmental Defense Fund

257 Park Avenue South
New York, NY 10010
Phone: 212-505-2100   Fax: 212-505-2375
Frederic D. Krupp, Executive Director

Purpose: Using science and law to develop and promote creative solutions to environmental problems.

Founded: 1967
FYR: 1991
Revenue: $18,546,109
Expenditures: $14,156,482
1990 membership: 220,000
Staff: 125

Topics: All environmental, but especially air quality, climate change, habitats, incineration, solid waste, wildlife

Approaches: Education, litigation, lobbying, policy, research

Scope: National

Special projects: Antarctica, Global Climate Change, Clean Air Act

Periodicals: *EDF Letter* (newsletter)

Books: Yes

Reports: Yes

Environmental Exchange

1930 18th Street, NW
Washington, DC 20009

Phone: 202-387-2182   Fax: 202-332-4865
Richard Wiles, Executive Director
Purpose: To identify effective grassroots environmental programs
    nationwide. The Exchange evaluates programs and acts as a
    clearinghouse for groups looking for models to emulate.
Founded: 1991
FYR: 1991
Revenue:[$350,000]
Expenditures: [$350,000]
Staff: 7
Topics: All environmental
Approaches: Education, grassroots organizing, publications,
    research
Scope: National
Periodicals: *Action Exchange* (newsletter)

Environmental Law Institute

1616 P Street, NW, Suite 200
Washington, DC 20036
Phone: 202-328-5150   Fax: 202-328-5002
J. William Sutrell, President
Purpose: To advance environmental protection by improving
    law management and policy. ELI researches a range of prob-
    lems, educates professionals and citizens, and convenes all
    sectors to work out solutions.
Founded: 1969
FYR: 1990
Revenue: Not available
Expenditures: Not available
Staff: 65
Topics: Conservation, environmental protection, wetlands
Approaches: Conferences, education, publications, research
Scope: International
Special projects: Eastern Europe Law and Legislation, State
    Superfund Study
Periodicals: *Environmental Law Reporter* (newsletter), *Environ-
    mental Forum* (magazine), *National Wetlands Newsletter*
Books: Yes
Reports: Yes

Environmental Support Center
1731 Connecticut Avenue, NW
Washington, DC 20009
Phone: 202-328-7813   Fax: 202-265-0492
James Abernathy, Executive Director
Purpose: To provide technical support for regional, state, local, and grassroots organizations working on environmental issues.
Founded: 1990
FYR: 1990
Revenue: [$645,000]
Expenditures: Not available
Staff: 5
Topics: All environmental
Approaches: Conferences, education, grassroots organizing, technical assistance, training
Scope: National

Friends of the Earth
218 D Street, SE
Washington, DC 20003
Phone: 202-544-2600   Fax: 202-543-4710
Michael S. Clark, President
Purpose: Originally founded by Sierra Club-renegade David Brower, FOE recently merged with the Oceanic Society and the Environmental Policy Institute. FOE espouses nonviolent activism to attain its broad goals of natural resource preservation.
Founded: 1969
FYR: 1989
Revenue: $3,023,969
Expenditures: $2,979,458
1990 membership: 50,000
Staff: 40
Affiliates: 40
Topics: All environmental, but especially biotechnology, business accountability, climate change, coastal issues, hazardous substances, international lending institutions, marine biodiversity, mining, nuclear issues, social justice, sustainable agriculture, waste, water quality

Approaches: Advocacy, conferences, education, funding, grass-
roots organizing, litigation, lobbying, policy, publications,
research
Scope: International
Special projects: Environmental consequences of war, environ-
mental justice
Periodicals: *Atmosphere* (newsletter), *Community Plume* (newslet-
ter), *Friends of the Earth* (magazine), *Groundwater News*
Books: Yes
Reports: Yes

Greenpeace USA
1436 U Street, NW
P.O. Box 3720
Washington, DC 20009
Phone: 202-462-1177   Fax: 202-462-4507
Peter Bahouth, Executive Director
Purpose: Greenpeace USA is part of a hugely successful interna-
tional grassroots organization working through direct action
to preserve the Earth and the life it supports.
Founded: 1971
FYR: 1990
Revenue: $33,102,299
Expenditures: $31,102,299
1990 membership: 2,350,000
Staff: 250
Chapters: 6
Topics: All environmental, but especially climate change,
endangered species, fisheries, marine issues, marine mam-
mals, military issues, nuclear issues, toxics
Approaches: Direct action, education, grassroots organizing,
lobbying, publications, research
Scope: International
Special projects: Cancel Trident 2 Missile Program, Stop Nuclear
Arms Race
Periodicals: *Greenpeace Magazine*
Reports: Yes

Institute for Local Self-Reliance
2425 18th Street, NW

Washington, DC 20009
Phone: 202-232-4108   Fax: 202-332-0463
Neil M. Seldman and David Morris, Co-Directors
Purpose: To provide economic and policy analysis to encourage conservation and sustainable, environmentally sound patterns of consumption and production.
Founded: 1974
FYR: 1990
Revenue: [$566,000]
Expenditures: [$506,000]
Staff: 16
Topics: All environmental, but especially energy efficiency, hazardous substances and waste, recycling, resource recovery, source reduction
Approaches: Conferences, grassroots organizing, media, publications, research, technical assistance
Scope: International
Special projects: Comprehensive Statewide Materials Policy (pilot projects in New Jersey and Minnesota), Models for Economic Development (using recycled materials)
Periodicals: *Fact to Act On* (fact sheets)
Reports: Yes

Island Press
1718 Connecticut Avenue, NW
Washington, DC 20009
Phone: 202-232-7933   Fax: 202-234-1328
Charles Savitt, President and Publisher
Purpose: To publish state-of-the-art books on conservation and the environment for environmental professionals as well as for academic, governmental, and lay audiences.
Founded: 1979
FYR: 1990
Sales: [$1,700,000]
Staff: 20
Affiliates: Center for Resource Economics
Topics: All environmental
Approaches: Education, publications, research
Scope: Global
Books: Yes

The Izaak Walton League of America
1401 Wilson Boulevard, Level B
Arlington, VA 22209
Phone: 703-528-1818   Fax: 703-528-1836
Donald Freeman, President
Purpose: Initially a sportsmen's organization, the League works through citizen involvement for water quality, protection of public lands, and restriction of wildlife populations. Outdoor ethics is a special focus.
Founded: 1922
FYR: 1990
Revenue: $1,757,546
Expenditures: $1,793,441
1990 membership: 50,000
Staff: 22
Chapters: 400
Topics: All environmental, but especially endangered lands, endangered species, environmental ethics, environmental protection, fisheries, natural resources, recreation, water quality
Approaches: Conferences, education, publications
Scope: National
Periodicals: *Outdoor America* (magazine), *Outdoor Ethics* (newsletter), *Splash* (newsletter)
Books: Yes
Reports: Yes

The Keystone Center
Box 606
Keystone, CO 80435
Phone: 303-468-5822   Fax: 303-262-0152
Robert W. Craig, President
Purpose: A conflict-management organization with a field-service component for youth and adults. The Center offers consensus-building approaches to controversial public-policy issues at local, state, national, and international levels. Recent environmental topics: Antarctica, biodiversity, biotechnology, sustainable development, and climate change.
Founded: 1975

FYR: 1990
Revenue: $3,538,200
Expenditures: $3,281,241
Staff: 28
Topics: All environmental
Approaches: Dispute resolution, education, publications
Scope: International
Periodicals: *Consensus* (newsletter)

League of Conservation Voters
1707 L Street, NW, Suite 550
Washington DC 20036
Phone: 202-785-8683   Fax: 202-835-0491
Bruce Babbitt, President
Purpose: Tracking members of Congress in their votes on environmental issues so that citizens can differentiate between opportunists and "real" environmentalists and know where to place their votes.
Founded: 1970
FYR: 1990
Revenue: [$1,000,000]
Expenditures: [$330,000]
1990 membership: 30,000
Staff: 11
Topics: All environmental
Approaches: Advocacy, policy
Scope: National
Periodicals: *Greengram* (newsletter), *LCV National Environmental Scorecard* (annual)

National Audubon Society
950 Third Avenue
New York, NY 10022
Phone: 212-832-3200   Fax: 212-593-6254
Peter A. A. Berle, President
Purpose: One of the best established mainstream environmental groups, Audubon works to preserve America's natural resources and encourage their wise use. Audubon has a strong local presence throughout the country and its 512 chapters

exercise a good deal of autonomy. Audubon's problems have recently been written up in the national press: Like other giant "nationals" of the environmental movement, it is struggling to maintain its share of the environmental pie.

Founded: 1886
FYR: 1990
Revenue: $37,450,497
Expenditures: $35,800,312
1990 membership: 548,523
Staff: 395
Chapters: 512
Topics: All environmental, but especially forests, habitats, natural resource conservation, nature centers, rivers/streams, wildlife
Approaches: Education, legislation, lobbying, policy, publications, research
Scope: National
Special projects: Arctic National Wildlife Refuge, Ancient Forests, Wetlands, Platte River
Periodicals: *Audubon* (magazine), *Audubon Activist* (newsletter)
Books: Yes
Reports: Yes

Natural Resources Defense Council

40 West 20th Street, 11th Floor
New York, NY 10011
Phone: 212-727-2700   Fax: 212-727-1773
John H. Adams, Executive Director
Purpose: One of the most influential of the nationals, NRDC uses law and the regulatory process to shape public policy on a wide range of environmental issues.
Founded: 1970
FYR: 1991
Revenue: $17,471,078
Expenditures: $17,654,076
1990 membership: 170,000
Staff: 150
Topics: All environmental
Approaches: Advocacy, education, litigation, lobbying, policy, publications, research

Scope: National
Special projects: National Alternative Energy Strategy, *Looking for Oil in All the Wrong Places*
Periodicals: *The Amicus Journal* (magazine)
Books: Yes
Reports: Yes

Renew America

1400 16th Street, NW, Suite 710
Washington, DC 20036
Phone: 202-232-2252   Fax: 202-232-2617
Tina Hobson, Executive Director
Purpose: To gather information on U.S. environmental problems and what's being done about them. Through its Environmental Success Index and Searching for Success programs, Renew identifies programs and projects that work.
Founded: 1978
FYR: 1990
Revenue: $652,000
Expenditures: $596,423
1990 membership: 4,000
Staff: 9
Topics: All environmental
Approaches: Conferences, demonstration projects, education, publications
Scope: National
Special projects: Environmental Success Index (annual)
Books: Yes
Reports: Yes

Resources for the Future

1616 P Street, NW
Washington, DC 20036
Phone: 202-328-5000   Fax: 202-939-3460
Robert W. Fri, President
Purpose: Originally funded by the Ford Foundation, Resources for the Future (RFF) conducts research on natural resources, especially in relation to economic issues, national policy, efficient use, cost-benefit analysis, and risk assessment. RFF looks at long-term resource trends such as energy

supply and at immediate problems such as agricultural poli-
cy or groundwater contamination.
Founded: 1952
FYR: 1990
Revenue: $7,151,712
Expenditures: $7,799,009
Staff: 105
Chapters: 4
Topics: All environmental, but especially natural resource policy
Approaches: Education, policy, publications, research
Scope: National
Periodicals: *Resources* (newsletter)

Scientists' Institute for Public Information
355 Lexington Avenue, 16th Floor
New York, NY 10017
Phone: 212-661-9110   Fax: 212-599-6432
Alan McGowan, President
Purpose: To provide a comprehensive, balanced view of science
and technology. This distinguished and influential organiza-
tion works to bridge the gap between scientists and the media.
Founded: 1963
FYR: 1990
Revenue: [$1,700,000]
Expenditures: [$1,600,000]
Staff: 24
Topics: All environmental, but especially agriculture, energy,
hazardous substances, nuclear issues, population, sciences,
technology
Approaches: Conferences, education, media, policy, publications
Scope: International
Periodicals: *SIPIscope* (magazine)

Sierra Club
730 Polk Street
San Francisco, CA 94109
Phone: 415-776-2211   Fax: 415-776-0350
Michael Fischer, Executive Director
Purpose: To educate citizens how to explore, enjoy, protect, and

restore the wild places of the Earth, while encouraging the responsible use of ecosystems and natural resources. The Sierra Club's network of chapters and local groups supports grassroots activism nationwide.

Founded: 1892
FYR: 1990
Revenue: [$37,000,000]
Expenditures: [$37,000,000]
1990 membership: 645,000
Staff: 125
Chapters: 57
Affiliates: Sierra Club Legal Defense Fund
Topics: All environmental, but especially conservation, ecosystems, natural resources, recreation, stewardship
Approaches: Advocacy, education, grassroots organizing, lobbying, policy, publications
Scope: National
Special projects: Ancient Forests, Arctic National Wildlife Refuge, Energy Efficiency, National Energy Policy
Periodicals: *Sierra* (magazine), *National News Report* (newsletter)
Books: Yes
Reports: Yes

Sierra Club Legal Defense Fund
180 Montgomery Street
San Francisco, CA 94104
Phone: 415-627-6700   Fax: 415-627-6740
Fredric P. Sutherland, President
Purpose: To provide legal representation to environmental organizations working on public lands, wildlife, and habitat conservation.
Founded: 1971
FYR: 1990
Revenue: $9,565,897
Expenditures: $7,824,015
Staff: 85
Chapters: 7 regional offices
Topics: All environmental, but especially air quality, coastal issues, forests, habitats, public lands, water quality, wildlife

Approaches: Advocacy, dispute resolution, grassroots organizing, litigation, lobbying, policy, publications, research
Scope: National
Special projects: Ancient Forests of the Pacific Northwest, Endangered Species and Habitat, International Human Environmental Rights, Urban Air Quality
Periodicals: *In Brief* (newsletter)
Books: Yes
Reports: Yes

World Resources Institute
1709 New York Avenue, NW, 7th Floor
Washington, DC 20006
Phone: 202-638-6300   Fax: 202-638-0036
James Gustave Speth, President
Purpose: This influential research and policy organization works with governments, development organizations, the private sector, and environmental organizations on global environmental issues. Its current central focus is sustainability: how to reconcile economic growth with preservation of natural resources. WRI has identified six transitions it believes essential for a sustainable human society. The demographic transition toward stable populations is first on the list; the technical transition away from wasteful and polluting industries is second.
Founded: 1982
FYR: 1990
Revenue: $9,218,487
Expenditures: $8,867,190
Staff: 95
Topics: All environmental, but especially biodiversity, climate change, developing countries, energy, forests, pollution, sustainable economic development, technology
Approaches: Conferences, policy, publications, research, technical assistance
Scope: International
Special projects: *New World Dialog, Environmental Almanac, World Resources* (bi-annual)
Books: Yes
Reports: Yes

Worldwatch Institute
1776 Massachusetts Avenue, NW
Washington, DC 20036
Phone: 202-452-1999   Fax: 202-296-7365
Lester Brown, President
Purpose: To research and publish information on global environmental issues to shape public opinion, policy, and events.
Founded: 1974
FYR: 1990
Revenue: [$3,500,000]
Expenditures: [$3,500,000]
Staff: 32
Topics: All environmental
Approaches: Education, policy analysis, publications, research
Scope: International
Periodicals: *State of the World* (annual); *Worldwatch* (magazine)
Reports: Yes

❑ Foundation Funding

Grants for environmental purposes represent a small but important part of all philanthropic activities in the United States. In 1990, U.S. independent and community foundations gave a total of $7.08 billion for all purposes. An estimated five percent of this was earmarked for environmental programs.

Ten of the top environmental grant-making foundations and a summary of their awards for all environmental topics are listed here.

□   **ENVIRONMENTAL GRANT-MAKING FOUNDATIONS:**   □
               FUNDING FOR ENVIRONMENTAL PROJECTS 1990

Rank	Foundation	Number of Grants	Dollars Awarded
1	Richard King Mellon Foundation	15	23,573,476
2	John D. and Catherine T. MacArthur Foundation	101	23,299,137
3	The Pew Charitable Trusts	70	14,554,709
4	The Ford Foundation	140	12,933,761
5	The Rockefeller Foundation	85	10,913,360
6	The David and Lucile Packard Foundation	29	8,440,225
7	W. Alton Jones Foundation, Inc.	97	7,468,610
8	W. K. Kellogg Foundation	23	7,436,577
9	The Andrew W. Mellon Foundation	25	6,267,900
10	National Fish and Wildlife Foundation	69	5,955,100

Based on a sample of 213 U.S. private and community foundations that made 4,265 environmental grants totaling $267,001,129 in 1990, the following distribution by issue can be observed:

ENVIRONMENTAL GRANT-MAKING FOUNDATIONS
SUMMARY OF AWARDS BY ISSUE, 1990

Rank	Topic	Percent	Dollars Awarded
1	Endangered Lands	27	72,563,882
2	Environment (nonspecific)	19	50,132,474
3	Biodiversity	15	39,807,738
4	Energy	8	21,720,738
5	Water	7	19,145,332
6	Oceans	7	18,719,149
7	Agriculture	5	14,042,796
8	Toxics	4	11,546,504
9	Development	3	7,832,339
10	Climate/Atmosphere	3	7,389,319
11	Waste	2	4,100,858

2

Population

THE HUMAN SPECIES HAS BEEN SO overwhelmingly successful—largely because of its skill in manipulating the Earth's natural resources—that its numbers now threaten the natural resource base itself.

As of January 1992, the human population numbered 5.4 billion and was growing by three people every second, or a quarter of a million people every day. It is estimated that about 100 million people will be added every year during the 1990s, so that by the year 2000 the world will contain the equivalent of a whole extra China. World population is expected to reach between 11.5 billion and 14 billion before leveling off sometime in the twenty-first century.

These numbers will come as a surprise to anyone who remembers learning a decade or so ago that the population problem was under control. Indeed, population growth *rates* have stabilized. Overall, the growth rate has fallen from its peak in the late 1960s; the 33 more developed countries (MDCs) today have an average growth rate of only 0.5 percent, and a few of them have achieved zero or even negative population growth. But worldwide population *growth* continues. The reason is "age structure," a factor that describes how a given population is distributed across different age brackets: 0–10 years, 10–20 years, and so on.

The 33 MDCs have an age structure that is essentially flat, except for slight bulges representing the baby boom (the 30–40 year olds) and the elderly. The median age in the MDCs is about 33 years. The 142 less developed countries (LDCs), however, have an age structure that bulges hugely in the younger brackets. The median age for those countries is about 21 years (in Africa, it is just 17).

A younger population means that there are more women of childbearing age, and that there will continue to be great numbers in the reproductive age group (15–45) for the next 30 years or so. As a result, the LDCs have an average growth rate of 2.1 percent—over four times that of MDCs. Some individual countries of sub-Saharan Africa have rates as high as 3.8 percent.

So even though many MDCs have halted population growth, and some LDCs (particularly China) have made notable progress in rate reduction, the population explosion continues. And because the LDCs already constitute 77 percent of the world's population (4 billion people), the balance of population is shifting among nations and geographic regions.

In 1950, Europe and North America contained 22 percent of the world's population; in 2025, they will have less than 9 percent. Africa, with 9 percent of the world's population in 1950, will account for more than 18 percent in 2025. The countries of eastern and southern Asia—India, China, Pakistan, and Bangladesh—already contain 42 percent of the world's population and will continue to dominate world population trends. With more and more of the world's people concentrated in what are often its poorest areas, already painful shortages of food, water, shelter, and sanitation will only become more severe.

FOOD. In 1990, even though the world produced enough food for all its people, at least 500 million were inadequately nourished—largely because of uneven distribution. In the future, there will also be actual shortages in food supply.

Already in the late 1980s, food production was losing ground to population, particularly in the LDCs. During the 1980s, per capita cereal production declined in 51 and rose in just 43 of the 94 LDCs tracked by the United Nations Food and Agriculture Organization. Some current estimates predict that by the year 2000, 36 countries with a combined population of 486 million will be unable to feed their own populations.

Environmental factors will make it difficult to compensate by increasing food production. Each year, the world loses 24 billion tons of topsoil through poor agricultural practices. Much more agricultural land is damaged by the salinization that results from overirrigation. Widespread deforestation and the potential impacts of climate change—in particular global warming and stratospheric ozone depletion—are also likely to take a toll on crop production. All told, these and other environmental factors are already reducing cereal production by 14 million metric tons (about 1 percent of total yield) per year. Yet we would have to produce 28 million more tons of grain per year just to keep pace with projected population growth.

SHELTER. At present, LDCs are mainly rural, but their urban populations are growing by 3.6 percent annually—over 400 percent faster than urban growth in MDCs and 60 percent faster than rural growth in LDCs. By the late 1980s, 72 percent of the new LDC urban dwellers lived in shanties or slums. Africa had the worst situation, with 92 percent of its new urban population underhoused.

WATER RESOURCES. Population growth is also exceeding LDCs' abilities to provide such services as safe drinking water, sanitation, and wastewater disposal. Between 1970 and 1988, the number of LDC urban households without safe water grew from 138 million to 215 million while those without sanitary facilities more than tripled from 98 million to 340 million. Wastewater treatment is rare in the LDCs. In Latin America, for example, as little as 2 percent of total urban sewage is treated. As burgeoning urban populations congregate in larger cities, shortages of food, water, housing, and sanitation facilities are worsening.

SOLUTIONS

Population is a complex, highly political issue. Perhaps because it is so closely linked with individual and species survival, any discussion of population control tends to engender extremist sentiments. Rational consideration of the issue also tends to be obscured by tangential factors such as the abortion controversy.

Even among the many groups that directly address the population problem, there is no consensus about the best approach. There are, in fact, three broad ways of thinking about the problem. These can be called the population rate approach, the development approach, and the resources approach.

The *population rate approach* looks at the various rates that affect population growth (births, deaths, migration, and so on) to project future trends. It largely ignores the influence of other factors such as natural resource availability, technical innovation, or capital growth. The population rate approach seeks to solve the population problem by lowering birth rates. The technique of choice is family planning, with contraceptive use as the standard of success. According to this standard, family planning programs have been highly successful: The use of contraceptives among married women in LDCs has increased from 8 percent in 1965 to more than 50 percent in 1991.

Critics of this approach argue that we do not know to what extent family-planning programs actually cause lower fertility and birth rates. A 1983 World Bank study suggests, for instance, that such programs may account for only 13 to 30 percent of the recent declines in fertility observed in developing countries.

The *development approach* is the method favored by the multilateral lending agencies. This view asserts that development itself will slow population growth, presumably by offering women alternatives to childbearing for satisfaction and security. The development approach uses what occurred at the time of the Industrial Revolution as its model. When Europe industrialized, advances in medicine and material comforts first led to a lower death rate and a consequent increase in population growth. But soon, as more people moved from the land to the cities, birth rates fell—presumably because there was less of a need for children in the urban work environment—and population growth rapidly stabilized.

Until just a few years ago, many demographers postulated a cause-and-effect relationship between industrial development and lower birth rates that they call the "demographic transition." They assumed that the same pattern would occur throughout the world. But the demographic transition has not occurred as uniformly as expected. Most of the LDCs of Africa, Asia, and Latin America experienced a dramatic drop in death rates, thanks to modern measures of sanitation and health received from the United States and other industrialized nations after World War II. The vaccines and drugs reduced infant mortality and helped people live longer. But birth rates in many of these countries have not declined. The resulting large and persistent discrepancy between birth and death rates has created the present exorbitant rate of population growth now seen throughout the developing world. Moreover, birth rates dropped in some of these countries even before development; in others (such as the Muslim countries), they have not dropped, even with development. The demographic transition theory, then, is not a simple solution.

The third or *resource approach* sets population issues within a larger ecological context. According to Paul and Anne Ehrlich, what matters most is the relationship between a population and the resource base that supports it. If a population cannot be sustained without depleting the resource base and degrading the environment, an area is overpopulated.

Whereas much of the attention on population issues is focused on poverty, the Ehrlichs argue that affluence is the key problem. The impact of a population on the environment then results from three factors: (1) the size of the population; (2) affluence, measured as the amount of natural resources the average person consumes; and (3) technology, or the environmental disruption involved in producing or disposing of the goods consumed: Environmental impact = Population x Affluence x Technology.

Per capita commercial energy is an index for affluence and technology—that is, for measuring the environmental damage and resource consumption of the average citizen in a given country. Hence, a baby born in the United States represents twice the destructive impact on the Earth's ecosystems and resources as one born in Sweden, 3 times that for one born in

Italy, 13 times that in Brazil, 35 times that in India, 140 times that in Bangladesh or Kenya, and 280 times that in Chad, Rwanda, Haiti, or Nepal.

Clearly the resource approach to the population problem is in direct conflict with the development approach. It's difficult to imagine a society undergoing the social changes needed to lower fertility rates—achieving better nutrition, sanitation, basic health care, education, and equal rights for women—that doesn't also crave the amenities bought with greater resource use.

The best approach to the population problem is doubtless some combination of the three approaches outlined here: slowing population rates, fostering economic development, and giving much greater attention to resource use. The problem is so immense that we must marshal all possible forces to deal with it. Funding is a major issue.

The World Bank estimates that the developing countries now spend a total of $3 billion each year on family planning and related activities, of which other nations provide about $600 million. As population scientists Steven W. Sinding and Sheldon J. Segal wrote in the *New York Times* on December 19, 1991, "If the U.N. projection of a world population of six billion by 1999 is not to be exceeded, the people in developing countries will require 44 billion condoms, 9 billion cycles of oral contraceptives, 150 million sterilization operations and 310 million intrauterine devices or Norplant insertions. This means the annual cost of family planning programs in the third world will triple, to about $9 billion; contraceptives alone will cost $400 million to $500 million a year."

The United States was the primary contributor to global population efforts until the Reagan administration cutbacks in 1984. It must take the lead again so that this most important of all the environmental problems can be at least somewhat controlled.

RESOURCES

☙ Books and Reports

The Effects of Family Planning Programs on Fertility in the Developing World. Nancy Birdsall, editor. World Bank Staff Working

Papers Number 677. Population and Development Series Number 2. Washington, DC: The World Bank. 1985, 206 pp.

The Global Politics of Abortion. Jodi L. Jacobsen. Worldwatch Paper 97. Washington, DC: Worldwatch Institute. July 1990, 69 pp.

The Population Explosion. Paul R. Ehrlich and Anne H. Ehrlich. New York: Simon & Schuster. 1990, 319 pp.

Population Pressure, the Environment and Agricultural Intensification: Variations on the Boserup Hypothesis. Uma Lele and Steven W. Stone. Washington, DC: The World Bank. 1989, 79 pp.

Population and Resources in a Changing World. Kingsley Davis, Mikhail S. Bernstam, and Helen M. Sellers, editors. Stanford, CA: Morrison Institute for Population and Resource Studies, Stanford University. 1989, 530 pp.

Population and Resources in Western Intellectual Traditions. Michael S. Teitelbaum and Jay M. Winter, editors. New York: Cambridge University Press. 1989, 309 pp.

The State of World Population 1991. Nafis Sadik. New York: United Nations Population Fund (UNPF). 1991, 48 pp.

Women's Reproductive Health: The Silent Emergency. Worldwatch Paper 102. Jodi L. Jacobson. Washington, DC: Worldwatch Institute. June 1991, 70 pp.

World Development Report 1991. New York: Oxford University Press for the International Bank for Reconstruction and Development/The World Bank. 1991, 344 pp.

World Population Projections, 1989-90 Edition: Short- and Long-Term Estimates. Rodolfo A. Bulatao, Eduard Bos, Patience W. Stephens, and My T. Vu. Baltimore: Johns Hopkins University Press for The World Bank. 1990, 421 pp.

❖ Organizations

Center for Population Options
1025 Vermont Avenue, NW, Suite 210
Washington, DC 20005

Phone: 202-347-5700   Fax: 202-347-2263
Judith Senderowitz, Executive Director
Purpose: To prevent teenage pregnancy by collaborating with other organizations.
Founded: 1980
FYR: 1990
Revenue: $2,046,505
Expenditures: $2,044,421
Staff: 26 (includes media)
Topics: Education, family planning, teenage pregnancy, youth
Approaches: Conferences, education, media, publications, research, technical assistance, training
Scope: International, but with a geographic focus on the United States and Latin America
Special projects: Life Planning Convention
Periodicals: *Options* (newsletter)
Reports: Yes

Centre for Development and Population Activities (CEDPA)
1717 Massachusetts Avenue, NW
Washington, DC 20036
Phone: 202-667-1142   Fax: 202-332-4496
Peggy Curlin, President
Purpose: To empower women at all levels of society to be full partners in development, and to enhance public awareness of current trends in population, resources, environment, and development.
Founded: 1975
FYR: 1990
Revenue: $3,315,263
Expenditures: $3,295,693
Staff: 6
Topics: Developing countries, development, family planning, health, nutrition, women
Approaches: Education, training, workshops
Scope: International
Special projects: The Better Life Project, Project Access, Nigeria Project
Periodicals: *CEDPA Worldwide* (newsletter)
Reports: Yes

Global Committee of Parliamentarians on Population Growth and Development
304 East 45th Street, 12th Floor
New York, NY 10017
Phone: 212-953-7947   Fax: 212-557-2061
Takeo Fukuda, President
Purpose: Working at the parliamentarian level to provide information and organizational resources that integrate population, maternal and child welfare, and environmental programs.
Founded: 1982
FYR: 1990
Revenue: $1,200,000
Expenditures: $1,200,000
Staff: 8
Topics: All population, but especially maternal and child health; all environmental
Approaches: Advocacy, conferences, education, policy
Scope: International
Periodicals: *Shared Vision* (newsletter)
Books: Yes
Reports: Yes

Alan Guttmacher Institute
111 5th Avenue
New York, NY 10003
Phone: 212-254-5656   Fax: 212-254-9891
Jeannie Rosoff, President
Purpose: To conduct research, policy analysis, and public education on reproductive health issues.
Founded: 1968
FYR: 1990
Revenue: [$4,000,000]
Expenditures: [$4,000,000]
1990 membership: 6,000
Change from 1989: +10%
Staff: 55
Affiliates: Planned Parenthood
Topics: All population, but especially abortion, family planning, sexual education, teenage pregnancy

Approaches: Advocacy, education, policy, publications, research
Scope: International
Periodicals: *Family Planning Perspectives* (journal), *International Family Planning Perspectives* (journal), *Washington Memo* (newsletter)
Books: Yes
Reports: Yes

International Women's Health Coalition
24 East 21st Street
New York, NY 10010
Phone: 212-979-8500   Fax: 212-979-9009
Joan B. Dunlop, President
Purpose: To improve women's reproductive health in the Third World.
Founded: 1980
FYR: 1990
Revenue: [$1,600,000]
Expenditures: [$1,600,000]
Staff: 12
Affiliates: Overseas Development Council
Topics: Developing countries, population
Approaches: Advocacy, conferences, education, funding, publications, research
Scope: International
Reports: Yes

National Abortion Rights Action League
1101 14th Street, NW, 5th Floor
Washington, DC 20005
Phone: 202-408-4600   Fax: 202-408-4698
Kate Michelman, Executive Director
Purpose: Viewing reproductive freedom more as an issue of women's self-determination than as population control, NARAL works to keep abortion safe, legal, and accessible. It focuses on electing pro-choice officials, legislators, and judges.
Founded: 1969
FYR: 1990

Revenue: $2,661,403
Expenditures: $2,264,662
1990 membership: 350,000
Staff: 36
Affiliates: 41 state organizations
Topics: Abortion, reproductive freedom
Approaches: Advocacy, education, grassroots organizing, legislation, litigation, policy, publications
Scope: National
Books: Yes
Reports: Yes

Negative Population Growth, Inc.
210 The Plaza
P.O. Box 1206
Teaneck, NJ 07666-1206
Phone: 201-837-3555   Fax: 201-837-0270
Donald W. Mann, President
Purpose: Works through public education to stabilize population at a sustainable level. NPG uses experts in various fields to analyze the effect of population growth on resources such as food and land use.
Founded: 1972
FYR: 1990
Revenue: $275,697
Expenditures: $258,242
1990 membership: 4,400
Staff: 3
Topics: Developing countries, natural resources, sustainability
Approaches: Education, policy, publications
Scope: International
Special projects: Study of Optimum Population Size
Periodicals: *Human Survival* (newsletter)
Reports: Yes

The Pathfinder Fund
Nine Gaten Street, Suite 217
Watertown, MA 02172
Phone: 617-924-7200   Fax: 617-924-3833

Daniel E. Pellegrom, Executive Director
Purpose: To increase the number of individuals in developing
    countries who have access to and who voluntarily use quality
    family-planning services.
Founded: 1957
FYR: 1990
Revenue: $14,682,750
Expenditures: $14,621,420
1990 membership: 3,500
Staff: 70
Topics: Developing countries, family planning
Approaches: Education, publications, research
Scope: International
Periodicals: *Pathways* (newsletter)
Reports: Yes

Planned Parenthood Federation of America, Inc.
810 Seventh Avenue
New York, NY 10019
Phone: 212-541-7800   Fax: 212-765-4711
Faye Wattleton, President
Purpose: With assistance from the U.S. Agency for International
    Development (U.S. AID), Planned Parenthood works to pro-
    mote access to voluntary reproductive health care services
    in more than sixty countries. This organization is now in the
    process of deciding whether to obey the new federal rule
    against abortion counseling or to forgo federal dollars.
Founded: 1916
FYR: 1990
Revenue: [$331,500,000]
Expenditures: [$321,200,000]
Staff: 11 (headquarters)
Topics: Abortion, education, family planning, reproductive free-
    dom
Approaches: Conferences, direct action, education, grassroots
    organizing, litigation, policy, publications, technical assis-
    tance
Scope: International
Books: Yes
Reports: Yes

The Population Council
1 Dag Hammarskjold Plaza
New York, NY 10017
Phone: 212-644-1300   Fax: 212-755-6052
George Zeidenstein, President
Purpose: Using biomedical, social, and health sciences research
to design family-planning programs for developing coun-
tries. More than half the Council's funding comes from gov-
ernment and the United Nations. An international staff
currently conducts programs in over forty countries.
Founded: 1952
FYR: 1990
Revenue: $35,557,205
Expenditures: $35,580,999
Staff: 225
Topics: Developing countries, education, family planning
Approaches: Conferences, education, funding, policy, publica-
tions, research, technical assistance, training
Scope: International
Periodicals: *Population and Development Review* (journal), *Studies
in Family Planning* (journal)
Books: Yes
Reports: Yes

Population Crisis Committee
1120 19th Street, NW, Suite 550
Washington, DC 20036-3605
Phone: 202-659-1833   Fax: 202-293-1795
J. Joseph Speidel, President
Purpose: Works to (1) disseminate information about popula-
tion to the public and policymakers and (2) support infor-
mation and supplies to family-planning programs in LDCs.
Founded: 1965
FYR: 1990
Revenues: $2,557,000
Expenditures: $2,455,000
Staff: 39
Topics: Developing countries, family planning
Approaches: Conferences, education, funding, media, policy,
publications, research, technical assistance

Scope: International

Special projects: Empowerment of women through credit in Bangladesh, testing new methods of birth control in Southern California and Mexico, female circumcision projects in Nigeria and Kenya, nonscalpel vasectomy, better treatment of incomplete abortions

Reports: Yes

The Population Institute

110 Maryland Avenue, NE

Washington, DC 20002

Phone: 202-544-3300   Fax: 202-544-0068

Werner Fornos, President

Purpose: To increase public awareness of world population growth, especially among the executive and legislative branches of the U.S. government. This organization works to build congressional and grassroots support for efforts to stabilize world population.

Founded: 1968

FYR: 1989

Revenue: $1,325,597

Expenditures: $1,389,314

1990 membership: 80,000

Staff: 15

Topics: Energy, environment, family planning, grassroots demonstrations, legislation

Approaches: Advocacy, conferences, education, grassroots organizing, legislation, policy, publications

Scope: International

Periodicals: *Popline* (newsletter)

Reports: Yes

Population Reference Bureau

1875 Connecticut Avenue, NW, Suite 520

Washington, DC 20009

Phone: 202-483-1100   Fax: 202-328-3937

Thomas W. Merrick, President

Purpose: To gather, interpret, and disseminate information about population trends and their implications.

Founded: 1929
FYR: 1990
Revenue: $2,998,771
Expenditures: $3,142,096
Staff: 40
Topics: Demography, environment
Approaches: Education, legislation, media, publications, research, technical assistance, training
Scope: International
Periodicals: *Population Bulletin* (newsletter), *Population Today* (newsletter)
Books: Yes

Population Resource Center

15 Roszel Road
Princeton, NJ 08540
Phone: 609-452-2822   Fax: 609-452-0010
Jane S. De Lung, President
Purpose: To act as a link between the demographic research community and policymakers in analyzing the impact of population trends on domestic and international issues.
Founded: 1975
FYR: 1990
Revenue: $1,114,000
Expenditures: $1,000,000
Staff: 9
Topics: Demography, developing countries, family planning
Approaches: Conferences, education, policy, publications, research
Scope: International
Special projects: Revision of "America in the 21st Century" information booklets
Reports: Yes

Population-Environment Balance, Inc.

1325 G Street, NW, Suite 1003
Washington, DC 20005
Phone: 202-879-3000   Fax: 202-879-3019
Rose M. Hanes, Executive Director

Purpose: Working from the grassroots to stabilize the U.S. popu-
lation in order to preserve the national resource base and
quality of life.
FYR: 1990
Revenues: $673,415
Expenditures: $649,079
Staff: 7
Topics: Carrying capacity, natural resources, population stabi-
lization
Approaches: Advocacy, education, grassroots organizing, policy,
publications
Scope: National
Periodicals: *Balance Report* (newsletter)
Reports: Yes

United Nations Population Fund
220 East 42nd Street
New York, NY 10017
Phone: 212-297-5000   Fax: 212-557-6416
Nafis Sadik, Executive Director
Purpose: To collect data, formulate and implement national
policy, and fund family-planning and maternal and child
health care programs in 141 LDCs.
Founded: 1969
FYR: 1990
Revenue: [$217,000,000]
Expenditures: [$217,000,000]
Staff: 250
Topics: Developing countries, environment, family planning,
health care
Approaches: Conferences, education, funding, publications,
research, technical assistance, training
Scope: International
Periodicals: *UNFPA Newsletter, Populi* (journal)
Books: Yes
Reports: Yes

Zero Population Growth, Inc.
1400 16th Street, NW, Suite 320

Washington, DC 20036
Phone: 202-332-2200   Fax: 202-332-2302
Katherine Janeway, President
Purpose: To promote zero population growth as *the* way to maintain the Earth's resources and sustain the quality of life.
Founded: 1968
FYR: 1990
Revenue: $1,656,921
Expenditures: $1,643,736
1990 membership: 23,000
Staff: 25
Topics: Conservation, natural resources, population stabilization, sustainability
Approaches: Conferences, education, grassroots organizing, legislation, lobbying, media, policy, publications
Scope: National
Periodicals: *The ZPG Reporter* (newsletter)
Books: Yes

3

Agriculture

WITH THE INVENTION OF AGRICUL-
ture in about 8000 B.C., human beings began to take control of
their environment. They replaced natural flora with crops and
were thus able to ensure the dependable food supply required
for proliferation of the species. Today, we have created "industrial agriculture," which carries manipulation of the environment to its limits. In so doing, we have created a long list of
environmental problems.

The United States is the world's model for industrial agriculture, characterized by its use of fossil fuel-based energy to produce huge crops of a single species. Although it results in high
crop yields, industrial agriculture is hard on the environment. It:

- Wastes energy
- Reduces genetic diversity
- Depletes and degrades water supplies
- Threatens human health
- Degrades soils
- Destroys wetlands

A further problem associated with modern agriculture—but perhaps not directly caused by it—is the ongoing conversion of prime farmland to other uses.

ENERGY. Worldwide, agriculture now consumes about 8 percent of total oil output; in the United States agriculture accounts for 17 percent of total energy use—at least seven times the amount used in 1950. (Energy includes production of pesticides and fertilizers as well as machinery operation.)

Industrial agriculture squanders energy: On average, ten units of nonrenewable fossil fuel energy yield a single unit of food energy. In contrast, subsistence farming generally can produce ten units of food for every unit of total energy expended. Thus 99 percent of the energy invested in industrial agriculture goes to waste.

GENETIC DIVERSITY. Although some 80,000 species of plants throughout the world are edible, only about 30 crops feed the world. Four crops—wheat, rice, corn, and potato—are most important. Since World War II there has been a worldwide trend away from crop rotation and toward monocropping—the continuous raising of a single crop, such as corn. Furthermore, plant breeding by large seed companies has resulted in the abandonment of local varieties of crops, and increased dependence on a few genetic strains.

Genetic uniformity is good for modern markets and farming techniques, but it makes crops highly vulnerable to pests and disease. American farmers learned the potential consequences of dependence on a single strain with the disastrous corn blight of 1970.

WATER DEPLETION AND DEGRADATION. Agriculture both depletes and degrades water supplies. Irrigation, especially as it is commonly practiced, uses vast quantities of water. Thirteen percent of U.S. cropland is irrigated. This irrigated land accounts for more than 30 percent of crops produced. It also accounts for 85 percent of the nation's consumptive water use. Irrigation practices are usually inefficient: On average, only 37 percent of the water used actually reaches the targeted plant.

Water pollution is perhaps the most damaging effect of agriculture. Agricultural runoff is the primary source of nonpoint pollution of rivers, streams, lakes, and estuaries. A recent study by the Environmental Protection Agency found that agricultural runoff impairs other in-stream uses of rivers and streams in forty-seven of the fifty states.

Irrigation often pollutes water by leading to salinization—a buildup of salts in the soil that occurs when water evaporates, leaving the salts behind. Salinization occurs on more than 1,000,000 acres a year, primarily in the arid and semi-arid parts of the world. In the United States, 25 to 35 percent of the irrigated land in the western states has become sufficiently saline to reduce productivity. Seven hundred thousand tons of salt wash into the Colorado River every year from the Grand Valley of western Colorado. The annual cost in reduced crop yield and equipment corrosion downstream is at least $50 million.

Agriculture accounts for more than 50 percent of suspended sediments from all sources discharged into surface waters. Between 675 million and 1.6 billion tons of eroded agricultural soils end up in U.S. waterways every year. Sediments block out the sunlight aquatic organisms need to survive. Sedimentation has enormous costs. In a 1985 report, The Conservation Foundation estimated the annual U.S. cost of sedimentation at $2.2 billion. The costs to society take many forms: flooding, damage to water treatment plants, the need for dredging, and lost recreational sites for swimming and fishing.

Nutrients such as phosphorus, nitrogen and potassium enter the soil from fertilizers and animal waste. When phosphorus is washed into surface waters, it overstimulates algal growth, leading to eutrophication of lakes and estuaries. Commercial fertilizer use in the United States peaked at about 23 million tons in 1981. Since then it has fallen to about 19 million tons. The National Research Council estimates that between 50 and 75 percent of the polluting nutrients in U.S. surface waters come from agricultural fertilizers and animal waste.

The use of pesticides has grown with the trend toward monoculture. Between 1940 and 1980, pesticide use increased tenfold. While such an increase might be justified by a reduction of the pest problem, crop losses from insects during the same period actually increased from 7 to 13 percent. In 1987, pesticides cost U.S. farmers $4 billion; 90 percent was used on four crops: corn, cotton, soybeans, and wheat.

HUMAN HEALTH. The U.S. Department of Agriculture estimates that the groundwater in 1,437 counties—46 percent of all agricultural counties—may be contaminated by agricultural fertilizers and pesticides.

Excessive intake of nitrates from nitrogenous fertilizers can lead to methemoglobinemia, a condition in which the oxygen-carrying capacity of blood is lowered. A 1986 survey by the U.S. Geological Survey (USGS) of 1,663 counties showed 474 in which 25 percent of the wells tested had elevated nitrate-nitrogen levels.

In 1988, pesticides were detected in the groundwater of twenty-six states, presumably due to agricultural runoff. In a 1989 survey of midwestern streams, the USGS found traces of pesticides in 90 percent of those tested. Pesticide exposure can cause a wide range of acute and chronic human health problems, including some cancers. Within the last few years, several studies have shown an increased incidence of certain cancers among farmers. A particular association was demonstrated between exposure to certain herbicides and non-Hodgkins lymphoma.

SOIL. The U.S. Soil Conservation Service estimates that about one-third of the original topsoil on U.S. croplands has already been washed or blown into rivers, lakes, and oceans. Wind and water erode between 2.7 and 3.1 billion tons of soil from U.S. cropland every year: an erosion rate seven times the rate of natural soil formation. The cost in plant nutrient loss is estimated to be $18 billion a year.

WETLANDS. Wetlands are one of the most valuable ecosystems. In particular, they are habitat for great numbers of species and act as natural filtration systems for polluted water.

The United States originally had 215 million acres of wetlands: only 90 million remain. Marshes, bogs, swamps, playas, prairie potholes, and other wetlands continue to disappear at a rate of 300,000 to 500,000 acres each year. Eighty percent of the loss of these wetland acres results from drainage to accommodate agricultural production.

LOSS OF FARMLAND. Although the total area of farmland in use has remained fairly constant, there is continuing pressure to convert farmland to housing developments, malls, and other uses. Based on USDA figures, American Farmland Trust estimates an annual loss of 2.1 million acres. Historically, towns arose near the most productive areas, so it is now prime farmland that is in greatest jeopardy, since it tends to lie adjacent to metropolitan centers.

The federal government has yet to act on the Farmland Protection Policy Act, part of the 1981 and 1985 farm bills. Meanwhile, state and local governments have stepped in: Nine states (and at least one county) in the Boston-Washington corridor have set up their own preservation programs.

SOLUTIONS

There are several ways to deal with the environmental problems created by modern agriculture. Among them are:

SUSTAINABLE AGRICULTURE. Sustainable agriculture is an evolving concept that defies simple definition. It is an approach to farming designed to save energy, conserve irrigation water and topsoil, and use fewer commercial fertilizers and pesticides. Sustainable agricultural techniques include crop rotation, polycropping, low or no tillage, trickle irrigation, use of legumes as nitrogen fixers, and integrated pest management (IPM), a technique which controls pests with a system of soil and biological strategies.

Low input sustainable agriculture (LISA)—recently renamed best utilization of biological applications (BUBA)—is a variation on sustainable agriculture. It is described as an attempt to reduce reliance on fertilizer, pesticides, and other purchased resources; to increase agricultural productivity and profits; to conserve energy and natural resources; to reduce soil erosion and loss of nutrients; and to develop sustainable farming.

But sustainable agriculture, LISA, and BUBA are all more than a collection of techniques. Implicit in each is an ethical dimension of the sort suggested by the pioneer of resource conservation, Aldo Leopold, in *A Sand County Almanac*:

> A land ethic . . . reflects the existence of an ecological conscience, and this in turn reflects a conviction of individual responsibility for the health of the land. Health is the capacity of the land for self-renewal. Conservation is our effort to understand and preserve that capacity.

Sustainable agriculture is no longer a fringe movement. In its sentinel 1989 report, *Alternative Agriculture*, the prestigious National Academy of Sciences urged that U.S. farmers adopt sustainable agriculture practices for both environmental and economic reasons. As of 1988, between 50,000 and 100,000 of the 650,000 U.S. farmers were using one or more sustainable agriculture practices. By 1990, more than 30 million acres (8 percent of U.S. farmland) were being managed under IPM programs. The net financial benefits were estimated at $500 million.

FEDERAL POLICY REFORMS. Most agricultural policy analysts agree that the environmental problems posed by U.S. industrial agriculture exist in great part because of our federal farm policy. According to the Congressional Budget Office, the agricultural industry receives more direct federal support than any other business sector. Farm program expenses peaked at $26 billion in 1983, but they are still high. In fiscal 1991, for example, total federal farm program outlays were $10.1 billion.

Financial incentives may be packaged as commodity price and income support programs, tax or credit policy, research programs, soil and water conservation programs, or EPA pesticide and water quality programs. All influence the farmer's choice of production methods and crops. Until very recently these incentives have been structured in a way that encourages monocropping and discourages crop rotation and other environmentally sound practices.

Every five years, the federal farm bill comes up for renewal, giving Congress a chance to review and restructure federal farm policy. In 1985, for the first time the farm bill contained several significant environmental provisions: in particular, the "conservation compliance" provision (requiring participating farmers to have conservation plans), the "sodbuster" provision (dealing with highly erodible lands), and the "swampbuster" provision (intended to preserve wetlands).

In 1990, as the result of an enormous effort by a host of groups including the National Audubon Society, American Farmland Trust, and the Institute for Resource Economics, the environmental agenda made even greater headway. Among the key provisions of the 1990 farm bill:

- *Water quality protection.* The 1990 act establishes a water quality incentive program, offering incentives and cost-sharing payments for farmers who implement methods that prevent pollution.

- *Soil protection.* The 1990 farm bill strengthens the "conservation compliance" provision of the 1985 farm bill, requiring farmers receiving commodity payments to have an approved conservation plan. It also broadens the Conservation Reserve Program, which takes highly erodible land out of production, and strengthens the "sodbuster" provisions designed to discourage the expansion of cropland into highly erodible soils.

- *Resource conservation.* The Integrated Farm Management Program allows farmers to plant resource-conserving crops in rotation with other crops without losing commodity benefits.

- *Wetland protection.* The 1985 wetland protection provision known as "swampbuster" was strengthened, and a new 1,000,000-acre wetland reserve program created.

- *Pesticide record keeping.* For the first time, farmers will be required to maintain records of their use of restricted pesticides.

- *Forestland protection.* A cost-sharing program will help landowners carry out forest management activities and protect environmentally important forests threatened by conversion to agricultural or other uses.

- *Sustainable agriculture research.* The tiny program for sustainable agriculture research and education authorized in 1985 was increased to $40 million a year.

All the environmental problems created by agriculture will certainly not be solved by this legislation, but at least federal policy is beginning to shift in the right direction.

RESOURCES

☙ Books and Reports

Agricultural Ecology. Joy Tivy. New York: John Wiley & Sons. 1990, 288 pp.

Agriculture and the Environment in a Changing World Economy. Washington, DC: The Conservation Foundation. 1986, 66 pp.

Alternative Agriculture. Washington, DC: National Academy Press. 1989, 417 pp.

The Environmental Scorecard for the 1990 Farm Bill. New York: Natural Resources Defense Council. 1991, 20 pp.

The Farm Fiasco. James Bovard. San Francisco: Institute for Contemporary Studies. 1991, 382 pp.

Farming in Nature's Image: An Ecological Approach to Agriculture. Judith D. Soule and Jon K. Piper. Foreword by Wes Jackson. Washington, DC: Island Press. 1992, 290 pp.

Green Fields Forever: The Conservation Tillage Revolution in America. Charles E. Little. Foreward by Norman Berg. Washington, DC: Island Press. 1987, 192 pp.

Harvest of Hope: Alternative Agriculture's Potential to Reduce Pesticide Use. New York: Natural Resources Defense Council. 1991, 120 pp.

New Roots for Agriculture. Wes Jackson. Lincoln, NE: University of Nebraska Press. 1985, 150 pp.

Paying the Farm Bill: Accounting for Environmental Costs of Agricultural Commodity Programs. Paul Faeth, Robert Repetto, Kim Kroll, Qu Dai, and Glenn Helmes. Washington, DC: World Resources Institute. 1991, 60 pp.

Reshaping the Bottom Line: On-Farm Strategies for a Sustainable Agriculture. David Granatstein. Lewiston, MN: Land Stewardship Project. 1988, 63 pp.

Shattering: Food, Politics, and the Loss of Genetic Diversity. Cary Fowler and Pat Mooney. Tucson, AZ: University of Arizona Press. 1990, 278 pp.

Soil and Survival: Land Stewardship and the Future of American Agriculture. San Francisco: Sierra Club Books. 1988, 217 pp.

The Violence of the Green Revolution: Ecological Degradation and Political Conflict. Vandane Shiva. Atlanta: Humanities Press International. 1991, 192 pp.

Water for Agriculture: Facing the Limits. Worldwatch Paper 93. Sandra Postel. Washington, DC: Worldwatch Institute. December 1989, 54 pp.

❂ Periodicals

American Farmland
American Farmland Trust
1920 N Street, NW, Suite 400
Washington, DC 20036
Phone: 202-659-5170   Fax: 202-659-8339
Tricia Obester, Editor
Type: Magazine
Frequency: Quarterly
Length: 12 pp.
Subscription fee: $15
Topics: Agricultural land preservation, agricultural policy, development, forests, open space, sustainable agriculture

Coverage: Organization activities, policy
Audience: Citizens, environmental organizations
Scope: National
Comment: Describes what this organization is doing to conserve the nation's agricultural resources, including efforts to preserve prime farmland.

American Journal of Alternative Agriculture
Institute for Alternative Agriculture, Inc.
9200 Edmonston Road, Suite 117
Greenbelt, MD 20770
Phone: 301-441-8777   Fax: 301-220-0160
I. Garth Youngberg, Editor
Type: Journal
Frequency: Quarterly
Length: 50 pp.
Subscription fee: $40
Topics: Alternative agriculture
Coverage: Book reviews, organization activities, policy, research
Audience: Business/industry, citizens
Scope: National
References: Yes
Comment: Articles about low-cost, resource-conserving, and environmentally sound farming practices.

Journal of Soil & Water Conservation
Soil and Water Conservation Society
7515 Northeast Ankeny Road
Ankeny, IA 50021-9764
Phone: 515-289-2331   Fax: 515-289-1227
Max Schnepf, Editor
Type: Journal
Frequency: Bimonthly
Length: 100 pp.
Subscription fee: $40
Topics: Hazardous substances, land use, nonpoint-source pollution, water quality and use
Coverage: Book reviews, legislation, organization activities, research
Audience: Business/industry, professional/academic

Scope: National
References: Yes
Comment: Technical, but not out of reach for the interested
   layperson, the *Journal* is dedicated to promoting the science
   and art of good land and water use.

Journal of Sustainable Agriculture
Food Products Press
10 Alice Street
Binghamton, NY 13904-1580
Phone: 607-722-5857
Raymond P. Poincelot, Editor
Type: Journal
Frequency: Quarterly
Length: 120 pp.
Subscription fee: $36
Topics: Sustainable agriculture
Coverage: Organization activities, policy, research
Audience: Citizens, professional/academic
Scope: International
References: Yes
Comment: Science and philosophy about sustainable
   agriculture.

The Land Report
The Land Institute
2440 East Well Water Road
Salina, KS 67401
Phone: 913-823-5376   Fax: 913-823-8728
Dana Jackson, Editor
Type: Newsletter
Frequency: 3 issues per year
Length: 35 pp.
Subscription fee: $15
Topics: Alternative agriculture, genetic diversity, land
   stewardship, polyculture, sustainable agriculture
Coverage: Book reviews, policy, research
Audience: Citizens, professional/academic
Scope: National

Comment: Chronicles activities at the Land Institute, particularly its work to research and demonstrate the practices of sustainable agriculture.

The New Farm
Rodale Press, Inc.
33 East Minor Street
Emmaus, PA 18098
Phone: 215-967-5171
George DeVault, Editor
Type: Magazine
Frequency: Bimonthly
Length: 60 pp.
Subscription fee: $15
Topics: Agricultural productivity, sustainable agriculture
Coverage: Business/industry, policy
Audience: Business/industry, citizens
Scope: National
Comment: Promotes a regenerative agriculture that "puts people, profit and biological permanence back into farming."

Small Farm Advocate
The Center for Rural Affairs
Box 405
Walt Hill, NE 68067
Phone: 402-846-5428
Nancy Thompson, Editor
Type: Newsletter
Frequency: Quarterly
Length: 15 pp.
Subscription fee: $15
Topics: Agricultural policy, development, family farms, farm size, rural affairs
Coverage: Legislation, litigation, organization activities
Audience: Business/industry, citizens, government
Scope: National
Comment: Reports on government policies affecting family-size farms. Includes information on bankruptcy, farm audit system, and rural development.

❖ Organizations

Agricultural Resources Center
115 W. Main Street
Carrboro, NC 27510
Phone: 919-967-1886
Allen Spalt, Director
Purpose: To perform research and public education on issues and policies related to safe food, family farm agriculture, and natural resource preservation. Special focus on reducing use of pesticides and developing alternative methods of pest control.
Founded: 1976
FYR: 1990
Revenue: $129,626
Expenditures: $121,332
Staff: 2
Topics: Family farms, pesticides, sustainable agriculture, traditional small-scale farms
Approaches: Education, publications, research
Scope: State (North Carolina)
Periodicals: *PESTed News* (newsletter)

American Farmland Trust
1920 N Street, NW, Suite 400
Washington, DC 20036
Phone: 202-659-5170   Fax: 202-659-8339
Ralph E. Grossi, President
Purpose: To protect prime U.S. farmland through land acquisition, education, and policy studies.
Founded: 1980
FYR: 1990
Revenue: $3,482,308
Expenditures: $3,155,416
1990 membership: 16,000
Staff: 12
Chapters: 3
Topics: Farmland preservation, soils, sustainable agriculture
Approaches: Conferences, education, grassroots organizing, land acquisition, lobbying, policy, publications, research

Scope: National
Periodicals: *American Farmland* (magazine)

The Center for Rural Affairs
Box 405
Walthill, NE 68067
Phone: 402-846-5428 Fax: 402-846-5428
Paul Olson, President
Purpose: To build sustainable rural communities in the United
 States and abroad that respect social and economic justice
 as well as our role as stewards for the natural environment.
Founded: 1973
FYR: 1990
Revenue: $1,457,347
Expenditures: $787,210
Staff: 19
Topics: Farm size, global warming, rural affairs, social justice,
 soils, stewardship, sustainable agriculture
Approaches: Advocacy, education, funding, publications,
 research
Scope: National
Special projects: Rural Economic Opportunities Program; Stew-
 ardship, Technology and World Agriculture Program
Periodicals: *Center for Rural Affairs* (newsletter)
Reports: Yes

Institute for Alternative Agriculture, Inc.
9200 Edmonston Road, Suite 117
Greenbelt, MD 20770
Phone: 301-441-8777 Fax: 301-220-0164
I. Garth Youngberg, Executive Director
Purpose: To encourage and facilitate the adoption of low-cost,
 resource-conserving, and environmentally sound farming
 methods.
Founded: 1983
FYR: 1990
Revenue: Not available
Expenditures: Not available
Staff: 4
Topics: Conservation, natural resources, sustainable agriculture

Approaches: Advocacy, conferences, education, lobbying, policy, publications, research
Scope: National
Periodicals: *Alternative Agricultural News* (newsletter), *American Journal of Alternative Agriculture* (journal)

International Alliance for Sustainable Agriculture
University of Minnesota
1701 University Avenue, SE
Newman Center, Room 202
Minneapolis, MN 55414
Phone: 612-331-1099   Fax: 612-379-1527
Terry Gips, President
Purpose: To promote sustainable agriculture food systems worldwide that are ecologically sound, economically viable, socially just, and humane.
Founded: 1983
FYR: 1990
Revenue: Not available
Expenditures: Not available
1990 membership: 800
Change from 1989: +18%
Staff: 3
Topics: Alternative pest management, social justice, sustainable agriculture
Approaches: Advocacy, education, grassroots organizing, lobbying, publications, research
Scope: International
Periodicals: *Manna* (newsletter)
Books: Yes

International Fund for Agricultural Research (IFAR)
1611 North Kent Street, Suite 600
Arlington, VA 22209
Phone: 703-276-1611   Fax: 703-525-1744
Floyd J. Williams, Executive Director
Purpose: To mobilize support for cooperative international agricultural research efforts.
Founded: 1985

FYR: 1990
Revenue: $1,457,347
Expenditures: $787,210
Staff: 4
Topics: Agriculture, international programs
Approaches: Collaboration, education, funding, research
Scope: International
Reports: Yes

The Land Institute
2440 E. Well Water Road
Salina, KS 67401
Phone: 913-823-5376   Fax: 913-823-8728
Wes Jackson, President
Purpose: To promote sustainable agriculture and a stewardship
    ethic for the preservation of prairie ecosystems. A central
    focus is the Institute's attempt to develop grain crops that
    are perennial rather than annual, and thus do not require
    yearly disruptions of the soil to plow and plant.
Founded: 1986
FYR: 1991
Revenue: $547,722
Expenditures: $512,163
1990 membership: 2,500
Staff: 12
Topics: Biodiversity, land stewardship, polyculture, prairies,
    soils, sustainable agriculture
Approaches: Demonstration projects, education, internships,
    publications, research
Scope: National
Periodicals: *The Land Report* (newsletter), *Land Letter* (newsletter)
Books: Yes

Land Stewardship Project
14758 Ostlund Trail, N
Marine on St. Croix, MN 55047
Phone: 612-433-2770   Fax: 612-433-2704
Ron Kroese, Executive Director
Purpose: To build support for land stewardship ethics and to

promote sustainable agriculture practices and policies through public education, grassroots organizing, participatory research and public policy initiatives.
Founded: 1982
FYR: 1989
Revenue: $598,662
Expenditures: $512,163
1990 membership: 5,817
Staff: 8
Affiliates: Sustainable Farming Association
Topics: Stewardship, sustainable agriculture
Approaches: Education, grassroots organizing, land acquisition, policy, publications, research
Scope: Regional (midwestern United States)
Special projects: Farmland Investor Accountability Program, Farmland Stewardship Center
Periodicals: *Land Stewardship Letter* (newsletter)
Reports: Yes

The Meadowcreek Project, Inc.
Meadowcreek Road
Fox, AR 72051
Phone: 501-363-4500   Fax: 501-363-4578
Luke Elliott, Director
Purpose: Education and research in alternative agriculture and energy for a sustainable economy. Meadowcreek offers internships to students of all ages and periodic conferences at its 1,500-acre farm.
Founded: 1979
FYR: 1990
Revenue: [$882,000]
Expenditures: [$160,000]
Staff: 10
Topics: Alternative agriculture, alternative energy, natural resources, rural development, social justice, sustainability
Approaches: Conferences, direct action, education, publications, research
Scope: National
Special projects: Environmental Education Center, internships

Periodicals: *Meadowcreek Notes* (newsletter)
Reports: Yes

Rodale Institute
222 Main Street
Emmaus, PA 18098
Phone: 215-967-5171   Fax: 215-967-6239
John Haberern, President
Purpose: A pioneer in the field of alternative agriculture, Rodale works to educate farmers and the public on issues such as the viability of the family farm and sustainable agriculture. The Institute maintains a large and varied research program.
Founded: 1947
FYR: 1990
Revenue: [$3,207,522]
Expenditures: [$3,207,522]
Staff: 50
Topics: Databases, demonstration programs, sustainable agriculture
Approaches: Advocacy, conferences, education, grassroots organizing, legislation, media, publications, research, technical assistance, training
Scope: International
Periodicals: *New Farm Magazine*
Books: Yes

Soil and Water Conservation Society
7515 Northeast Ankeny Road
Ankeny, IA 50021-9764
Phone: 515-289-2331   Fax: 515-289-1227
Verlon K. Vrana, Executive Vice-President
Purpose: To promote the wise use of land and water resources.
Founded: 1945
FYR: 1990
Revenue: $1,256,025
Expenditures: $1,145,977
1990 membership: 12,000
Staff: 16

Affiliates: World Association of Soil & Water Conservation
Topics: Soil conservation, water quality, water use
Approaches: Education, publications, research
Scope: International
Periodicals: *Conservagram* (newsletter), *Journal of Soil & Water Conservation*
Reports: Yes

The Wisconsin Rural Development Center, Inc.
Box 504
Black Earth, WI 53515
Phone: 608-437-5971
Don Rudolph, President
Purpose: To work for sustainability in rural Wisconsin, especially by supporting small and medium-size family-operated farms and by promoting sustainable agricultural practices.
Founded: 1983
FYR: 1990
Revenue: $189,358
Expenditures: $143,512
Staff: 8
Affiliates: Sustainable Agricultural Working Group
Topics: Alternative and sustainable agriculture, family farms, farm size, soils, stewardship
Approaches: Advocacy, collaboration, direct action, education, policy, publications, research
Scope: State (Wisconsin)
Special projects: Cultural Heritage
Periodicals: *Wisconsin Rural Development Center* (newsletter)
Reports: Yes

❏ *Foundation Funding*

In 1990, about 5 percent of the dollars awarded by U.S. independent and community foundations for environmental programs went for sustainable agriculture and related projects.

❑ **ENVIRONMENTAL GRANT-MAKING FOUNDATIONS:** ❑
FUNDING FOR AGRICULTURE PROJECTS 1990

Rank	Foundation	Number of Grants	Dollars Awarded
1	The Ford Foundation	39	2,818,410
2	Northwest Area Foundation	12	2,518,394
3	W. K. Kellogg Foundation	2	1,809,720
4	The Joyce Foundation	12	888,085
5	Jessie Smith Noyes Foundation, Inc.	16	813,000
6	The Rockefeller Foundation	7	692,700
7	Rockefeller Brothers Fund	7	545,000
8	Charles Stewart Mott Foundation	8	426,005
9	The Pew Charitable Trusts	5	425,000
10	John D. and Catherine T. MacArthur Foundation	6	367,700

4

Energy

MODERN INDUSTRIAL SOCIETY IS characterized by its use of huge quantities of energy. This energy use has a greater impact on the environment than any other single human activity.

It was the harnessing of fossil fuels—solar energy biologically transformed and stored for millions of years beneath the Earth's surface—that made the Industrial Revolution possible. Today, fossil fuels account for more than 90 percent of the world's commercial energy. They are also the most important source of environmental degradation. The combustion of coal, oil, and gas creates air pollution and acid rain that damage trees, crops, and aquatic life around the world. The use of fossil fuels is also the primary factor in the buildup of atmospheric greenhouse gases, believed to be causing climate change.

ENERGY USE

Worldwide, fossil fuel consumption has increased almost four times as rapidly as world population in the twentieth century.

The pattern of consumption is patchy, varying greatly from country to country. In general, the industrialized MDCs of the North use lots of fossil fuel energy; the LDCs use considerably less. For example, according to World Resources Institute, U.S. primary energy use per capita from all sources currently is about 280 gigajoules. This is in contrast to Europe, with a per capita energy use of about 130 gigajoules, and to the LDCs with a per capita energy use of only 21 gigajoules.

It has been said that there are three reasons why such fossil fuel dependence cannot continue:

- *Political reality.* The limited availability of fossil fuels: specifically, that two-thirds of the known petroleum reserves lie in the Persian Gulf.

- *Environmental reality.* The burden of pollution from a $20 trillion world economy run on fossil fuels that emits 6 billion tons of carbon to the atmosphere each year.

- *Social reality.* What is likely to happen as citizens come to understand the implications of the first two reasons.

The United States, with 4.8 percent of the world population, leads the pack of industrialized nations, using 25 percent of total world energy. We not only consume more than our share of energy, we also squander it through inefficiency. We use, for example, twice as much energy per dollar of gross national product (GNP) as Japan and several other industrialized nations.

Eighty-nine percent of U.S. energy comes from fossil fuels: 42 percent from oil, 24 percent from coal, 23 percent from natural gas. Nuclear sources contribute 7 percent; renewable sources such as hydropower, solar, photovoltaic, biomass, geothermal, and wind power account for the remaining 4 percent of energy consumption. The use of renewables in the United States lags behind the rest of the world, where renewables account for 20 percent of total energy production.

The use of nuclear energy in this country also contrasts with certain industrial nations. More than half of the energy generation for France, for instance, comes from nuclear power. Nuclear power, using the heat released in the fission (splitting) of uranium, produces no atmospheric pollutants. Most public concern is about the safety of the plants where the energy is generated, a problem that can be dealt with by scrupulous engineering design and practice. The fission products produced, however, are dangerous, hard to contain, and very long-lived. Whether these can and will be safely handled over their hundreds of years of hazardous life is the subject of serious debate.

Energy use in the United States is distributed among industry (36 percent), residential/commercial (36 percent), and transportation (28 percent).

The United States accounts for nearly one-fourth of world carbon dioxide emissions from fossil fuels. Within the United States, electric utilities are the largest source of carbon dioxide (35 percent), followed by transportation (30 percent), industry (25 percent), and residential/commercial (10 percent). The utilities are the biggest player because 60 percent of electricity is generated from coal. For each unit of energy obtained in combustion, coal emits 40 percent more carbon dioxide than oil and almost 100 percent more carbon dioxide than natural gas.

ENERGY EFFICIENCY

Energy efficiency could be greatly increased within each sector:

- *Utilities.* New electric-generation technologies could increase conversion efficiency from its present 33 percent to 45 percent. Least-cost planning that encourages efficiency can obviate the need for new plants. Under least cost, a utility must give equal consideration to supply-side options (building new plants) and demand-side options (enhanced energy efficiency). The utility then must choose the least expensive option, and costs include the environmental costs to consumers and society.

- *Transportation.* From 1974 to 1986, the fuel efficiency of new motor vehicles doubled, mainly because of increasing gasoline prices and two federal laws: the Corporate

Automotive Fuel Economy (CAFE) standard of 1975 and the gas-guzzler tax of 1979. Since 1986, there has actually been a decline in overall efficiency of the automotive fleet. We now use more fuel-inefficient light trucks and take more trips than ever. And the fuel-efficiency standard for new American cars in 1992 is still just 27 miles per gallon.

- *Industry.* Use of sensors and controls, better heat-recovery systems, and friction-reducing technologies can reduce industrial energy consumption by at least 40 percent. Cogeneration (the combined production of heat and energy) is especially promising. It now accounts for over 20 percent of total energy, and production is expanding rapidly.

- *Residential and commercial.* Greater efficiency will save 40 to 60 percent of energy used in old buildings, 70 to 90 percent of that used in new buildings. Available technologies include condensing furnaces that can cut energy use by 28 percent; better heating and cooling controls to cut energy use by 10 to 20 percent; more efficient lighting to cut use by 75 percent; and better insulation to cut use by 68 to 89 percent.

RENEWABLE ENERGY

Renewable energy sources are often considered innovative or untried: In fact, they date from the beginnings of human civilization. Indeed, it is the extensive use of fossil fuels that is very recent.

Renewables received a great deal of attention during the oil crisis of the 1970s and later because of growing concern about pollution. Federal subsidies for renewable energy research and development (R & D) increased nearly tenfold between 1975 and 1980. As a result, a great deal of progress was made in developing renewable technologies.

Although federal funding for renewables has fallen by over

80 percent since its peak in 1980, we are now at a point where several renewable energy technologies are sound and competitive. What we now need are the market incentives to put them in place.

- *Solar energy.* The price of photovoltaic cells, which convert sunlight directly to electricity, has dropped tenfold since 1976. Solar collectors, which use solar heat to warm water or air or to generate electricity, have also become competitive. In California several 30-megawatt solar-thermal electric plants supply electricity to utilities.

- *Wind power.* The average price of wind turbines is now about $1 per watt (25 percent that of photovoltaics). In 1987, California, the largest user of wind power, had 17,000 windmills producing 1,500 megawatts of electricity.

- *Geothermal power,* generated from heat in the Earth's interior, now produces 2,000 megawatts of power in the United States and 5,000 megawatts worldwide. The U.S. supply could grow tenfold by the year 2000. Geothermal power is at present limited to areas where steam or hot water can be extracted directly from the ground. But two new methods, "hot dry rock" (which involves deep drilling) and ocean thermal power (derived from a difference in water temperature at the ocean's surface and depths) are being developed.

- *Hydroelectric power and biomass* already supply 21 percent of world energy. But hydropower depends on the building of dams, which historically has caused enormous economic and environmental problems. Biomass energy traditionally involves the destruction of forests for fuel. This contributes to the greenhouse effect, soil erosion, rapid runoff, and silting of rivers. However, new types of biomass seem to have considerable potential. Wastes from forestry and agriculture, portions of the municipal waste stream, and specially grown crops can be used in various ways, including burning and conversion to liquid fuels through digestion or fermentation.

The United States made enormous gains in energy efficiency between 1973 and 1986 as a response to the Mid-East oil crisis. During this period, with greater efficiency, consumption remained almost constant while the economy expanded by 45 percent. As a result, we are now saving $150 billion a year. With the fall in oil prices after 1986, however, consumption began to rise again.

A huge amount of energy is still wasted each year. It has been estimated that with current technologies the MDCs could cut their per capita energy use by one-half and total energy use by one-third in thirty years. And the LDCs could raise their standard of living to the level Western Europe enjoyed in the 1970s just by adopting more efficient technologies for such things as cooking and lighting. With these changes, world energy consumption would be only slightly higher in 2020 than it is today and about half of what it is otherwise projected to be.

ENERGY POLICY

Through most of the twentieth century—with the exception of the mid-1970s—U.S. energy policy has been aimed at reliable and affordable fossil fuel supplies. The present administration carries on this tradition. Despite mounting evidence about global warming plus the reality of the Persian Gulf War, the Bush administration has refused to address the problem of demand.

The administration requested $182.6 million in its fiscal year (FY) 1991 budget for energy-efficiency R&D, a cut from the FY 1990 level of $194.1 million. Congress countered by appropriating $226 million, an increase of over 15 percent. The administration also tried to cut state and local conservation programs from $217.5 million to $30 million. Congress in turn mandated an increase to $268.3 million as well as a fifteen-month extension of the 10 percent tax credit for businesses installing solar- and geothermal-energy equipment.

In February 1991, at the height of battle in the Persian Gulf, the administration released its National Energy Strategy (NES). It was billed as a long-term, comprehensive policy that would guide us away from our dependence on foreign oil, toward new economic vigor and a healthier environment. But the NES did none of these, which would have been possible only through a systematic attempt to cut demand. Instead, its focus was again on increasing the supply of energy.

As summarized in the spring 1991 issue of *Nucleus,* published by the Union of Concerned Scientists:

> The National Energy Strategy is a deeply flawed plan. The major problems are its:
>
> - emphasis on increasing the energy supply rather than cutting demand through greater energy efficiency;
>
> - aim of drilling for oil in environmentally sensitive areas;
>
> - goal of quickly doubling nuclear power capacity;
>
> - tiny funding increases for R&D on renewable energy sources like solar, wind, and biomass, and huge increases for nuclear fission and fusion;
>
> - major funding cuts to important energy-conservation programs;
>
> - failure to substantially reduce greenhouse-gas emissions, principally CO_2;
>
> - failure to reflect the true environmental and public-health costs of energy.

This policy was promulgated despite nationwide hearings by the Department of Energy that demonstrated public concern about energy conservation and environmental protection.

The National Energy Security Act, introduced in 1991 by Senators Johnston (D-LA) and Wallop (R-WY), incorporated the philosophy of the White House energy strategy. In addition, it exempted certain energy supply projects from the provisions of several environmental laws. But the bill was never brought to a vote. Objections to oil drilling in the Arctic and the lack of conservation incentives were especially influential in its defeat.

RESOURCES

✄ Books and Reports

Advanced Light Vehicle Concepts. Amory B. Lovins. Snowmass, CO: Rocky Mountain Institute. 1991, 15 pp.

Alternatives to the Automobile: Transport for Livable Cities. Worldwatch Paper 98. Marcia D. Lowe. Washington, DC: Worldwatch Institute. October 1990, 49 pp.

Beyond the Petroleum Age: Designing a Solar Economy. Worldwatch Paper 100. Christopher Flavin and Nicholas Lenssen. Washington, DC: Worldwatch Institute. December 1990, 65 pp.

Building on Success: The Age of Energy Efficiency. Worldwatch Paper 82. Christopher Flavin and Alan B. Durning. Washington, DC: Worldwatch Institute. March 1988, 74 pp.

Cool Energy: The Renewable Solution to Global Warming. Michael Brower. Cambridge, MA: Union of Concerned Scientists. 1990, 89 pp.

Energy and the Ecological Economics of Sustainability. John Peet. Washington, DC: Island Press. June 1992, 300 pp.

Energy Efficiency: A New Agenda. William U. Chandler, Howard S. Geller, and Marc R. Ledbetter. Washington, DC: American Council for an Energy-Efficient Economy. 1988, 76 pp.

Energy for Development. Jose Goldemberg, Thomas B. Johansson, Amulya K. N. Reddy, and Robert H. Williams. Washington, DC: World Resources Institute. 1987, 73 pp.

Energy, the Environment, and Public Policy: Issues for the 1990s. David L. McKee, editor. Westport, CT: Greenwood Publishers. 1991, 220 pp.

"Energy for Planet Earth." *Scientific American* (entire issue). September 1990, 184 pp.

Energy for a Sustainable World. Jose Goldemberg, Thomas B. Johansson, Amulya K. N. Reddy, Robert H. Williams. Washington, DC: World Resources Institute. 1987, 119 pp.

Energy Unbound: A Fable for America's Future. L. Hunter Lovins, Amory B. Lovins, and Seth Zuckerman. San Francisco: Sierra Club Books. 1986, 390 pp.

Environmental Impacts of Renewable Energy: The OECD Compass Project. Paris: Organization for Economic Cooperation and Development (OECD). 1988, 93 pp.

Power Plays: Profiles of America's Independent Renewable Electricity Developers. Susan Williams and Kevin Porter. Washington, DC: Investor Responsibility Research Center. 1989, 456 pp.

The Renewable Energy Sourcebook. Laurie Burnham, Thomas B. Johansson, Henry Kelly, Amalya K. N. Reddy, and Robert H. Williams, editors. Washington, DC: Island Press. June 1992, 950 pp.

Renewable Energy: Today's Contribution, Tomorrow's Promise. Worldwatch Paper 81. Cynthea Pollock Shea. Washington, DC: Worldwatch Institute. 1988, 68 pp.

Resource Efficient Housing: An Annotated Bibliography and Directory of Helpful Organizations. Robert Sardinsky and The Rocky Mountain Institute. 1991, 161 pp.

Steering a New Course: Transportation, Energy, and the Environment. Deborah Gordon. Washington, DC: Island Press. 1991, 250 pp.

✪ Periodicals

EPRI Journal
Electric Power Research Institute
Environmental Control Systems Dept.
3412 Hillview Avenue
P.O. Box 10412
Palo Alto, CA 94303
Phone: 415-855-2000   Fax: 415-855-2954
David Dietrich, Editor
Type: Journal

Frequency: Monthly
Length: 56 pp.
Subscription fee: $29
Topics: Alternative energy, energy efficiency, energy policy, fossil fuels
Coverage: Business/industry, policy, research
Audience: Business/industry
Scope: National
Comment: A fine industry publication with some articles that are somewhat technical, others widely accessible and well worth reading on topics such as the national energy strategy and photovoltaics.

Geopolitics of Energy
Conant & Associates, Ltd.
1300 L Street, NW, Room 1200
Washington, DC 20005
Phone: 202-289-8970　　　Fax: 202-289-4866
Melvin A. Conant, Editor
Type: Newsletter
Frequency: 10 issues per year
Length: 10 pp.
Subscription fee: $325
Topics: Energy policy, energy supply, fossil fuels
Coverage: Business/industry, policy
Audience: Business/industry, government, professional/academic
Scope: International
Comment: Descriptive pieces, mainly on fossil fuel supply issues.

Home Energy
Energy Auditor & Retrofitter
2124 Kittredge Street, No. 95
Berkeley, CA 94704
Phone: 415-524-5405
Alan Meier, Executive Director
Type: Magazine
Frequency: Bimonthly
Length: 44 pp.

Subscription fee: $45
Topics: Energy efficiency, housing, renewable energy, utilities, waste reduction
Coverage: Business/industry, policy, research
Audience: Citizens
Scope: National
Comment: Useful information about residential energy conservation. Typical articles: "Do Reusable Diapers Use More Energy?" and "Passive Solar Design: Housewarming with Many Efficient Returns."

Independent Energy
Alternative Sources of Energy, Inc.
107 South Central Avenue
Milaca, MN 56353
Phone: 612-983-6892   Fax: 612-983-6893
Donald Marier, Editor
Type: Magazine
Frequency: 10 issues per year
Length: 56 pp.
Subscription fee: $64
Topics: Alternative energy sources, cogeneration, the Resource Conservation and Recovery Act (RCRA), resource recovery
Coverage: Business/industry
Audience: Business/industry
Scope: International
Advertising: Yes
Comment: On the premise that 60,000 to 100,000 megawatts of additional capacity will be needed by 2010, this publication argues for a growing role for the small energy generator.

The Journal of Energy and Development
International Research Center for Energy & Economic Development
Campus Box 263
University of Colorado
Boulder, CO 80309-0263
Phone: 303-492-7667   Fax: 303-442-5042
Dorothea H. El Mallakh, Managing Editor

Type: Journal
Frequency: Biannual
Length: 180 pp.
Subscription fee: $32
Topics: Development, energy consumption, energy supply, fossil fuels, nuclear power
Coverage: Book reviews, policy, research
Audience: Professional/academic
Scope: International
Comment: A fine scholarly journal. Recent articles: "Explaining the Decline of Nuclear Power in the United States" and "New Evidence on the Causal Relationship between United States Energy Consumption and Gross National Product."

Nucleus
Union of Concerned Scientists
26 Church Street
Cambridge, MA 02238
Phone: 617-547-5552   Fax: 617-864-9405
Steven Krauss, Editor
Type: Newsletter
Frequency: Quarterly
Length: 8 pp.
Subscription fee: Free with membership
Topics: Energy policy, nuclear power, radioactive waste, technology
Coverage: Book reviews, legislation, organization activities, research
Audience: Citizens, professional/academic
Scope: International
Comment: An outstanding newsletter covering energy policy and security with a special focus on nuclear issues.

❖ Organizations

Alliance to Save Energy
1725 K Street, NW, Suite 914
Washington, DC 20006-1401

Phone: 202-857-0666   Fax: 202-331-9588
Senator Timothy E. Wirth, Chairman
Purpose: A coalition of business, government, environmental, and consumer leaders working to increase the efficiency of energy use by the industrial, utility, and residential sectors.
Founded: 1977
FYR: 1990
Revenue: $1,363,403
Expenditures: $1,340,250
Staff: 14
Topics: Economic development, energy efficiency, global warming, national security
Approaches: Conferences, education, pilot projects, policy analysis, technical assistance
Scope: National
Periodicals: *Alliance Update* (newsletter)
Reports: Yes

The American Council for an Energy-Efficient Economy
1001 Connecticut Avenue, NW, Suite 535
Washington, DC 20036
Phone: 202-429-8873   Fax: 202-429-2248
Howard Geller, Executive Director
Purpose: To promote energy efficiency in buildings, equipment, and transportation and through research and analysis.
Founded: 1980
FYR: 1990
Revenue: [$1,000,000]
Expenditures: [$1,000,000]
Staff: 8
Topics: Energy efficiency
Approaches: Advocacy, conferences, education, publications, research
Scope: National
Special projects: Industrial Energy Efficiency, Transportation Energy Efficiency, National Energy Policy
Books: Yes
Reports: Yes

Biomass Users Network
P.O. Box 33308
Washington, DC 20033
Phone: 202-778-9665   Fax: 202-293-9211
Carlos Quesada, Executive Director
Purpose: To promote the use of biomass and biomass systems for developing countries. The primary objective is to identify opportunities for improving rural economies while protecting natural resources.
Founded: 1984
FYR: 1989
Revenue: $338,448
Expenditures: $247,626
Staff: 2
Chapters: 3
Affiliates: United Nations Environment Programme (UNEP), World Wildlife Fund (WWF), International Union for Conservation of Nature and Natural Resources (IUCN)
Topics: Biomass, conservation, development, natural resources
Approaches: Demonstration projects, education, information, technical assistance
Scope: International
Periodicals: *Network News* (newsletter)
Reports: Yes

The Center for Energy and Environmental Studies
The Engineering Quadrangle
Princeton University
Princeton, NJ 08544
Phone: 609-258-5445   Fax: 609-258-3661
Robert H. Socolow, Director
Purpose: An independent research unit of Princeton University's School of Engineering working to explore the potential of new technologies to solve environmental problems.
Founded: 1971
FYR: 1990
Revenue: $2,000,000
Expenditures: $2,000,000

Staff: 42
Topics: Energy efficiency, international security, military issues, technology
Approaches: Research
Scope: International
Periodicals: *Science and Global Security* (journal)
Reports: Yes

Citizens Coalition for Energy Efficiency
100 North 17th Street, 3rd Floor
Philadelphia, PA 19103
Phone: 215-563-3989   Fax: 215-563-3948
Benjamin Scott Hunter, Administrator
Purpose: To promote energy efficiency throughout the Delaware Valley.
Founded: 1980
FYR: 1990
Revenue: [$300,000]
Expenditures: [$300,000]
Staff: 9
Topics: Energy efficiency
Approaches: Advocacy, conferences, direct action, education, funding, grassroots organizing, policy, publications, research
Scope: Regional
Special projects: Energy Efficiency for Mushroom Growers, Reuse of Motor Oil
Periodicals: *The Delaware Valley Energy Report* (magazine), *Accent on Energy* (newsletter)
Books: Yes
Reports: Yes

Critical Mass Energy Project
215 Pennsylvania Avenue, SE, 3rd Floor
Washington, DC 20003
Phone: 202-546-4996   Fax: 202-547-7392
Lynn Bossong, Director
Purpose: To oppose nuclear power and promote safer energy alternatives.

Founded: 1971
FYR: 1990
Revenue: [$200,000]
Expenditures: [$200,000]
Staff: 7
Topics: Energy conservation, global warming, nuclear power
Approaches: Advocacy, education, publications, research
Scope: National
Periodicals: *Critical Mass Energy Bulletin* (newsletter)
Books: Yes
Reports: Yes

Environmental and Energy Study Institute
122 C Street, NW, Suite 700
Washington, DC 20001
Phone: 202-628-1400   Fax: 202-628-1825
Ken Murphy, Executive Director
Purpose: Set up by Congress to promote better informed national debate on environmental and energy issues, this group puts out reports and issue briefs for Capitol Hill, the executive branch, and others.
Founded: 1984
FYR: 1990
Revenue: $2,224,107
Expenditures: $2,080,831
Staff: 17
Topics: Clean Air Act, climate change, energy efficiency, sustainable development, waste management, water policy
Approaches: Conferences, education
Scope: National
Periodicals: *Weekly Bulletin* (newsletter)
Reports: Yes

International Institute for Energy Conservation, Inc.
420 C Street, NE
Washington, DC 20002
Phone: 202-546-3388   Fax: 202-546-6978
Deborah L. Bleviss, Executive Director

Purpose: To help developing countries plan programs for ener-
gy efficiency that will diminish the 80 percent increase in
energy demand projected to occur between 1985 and 2000.
Founded: 1984
FYR: 1990
Revenue: $691,312
Expenditures: $543,520
Staff: 18
Chapters: 3
Topics: Energy efficiency, fossil fuels, multilateral development
banks, problem-solving training, sustainable development,
transportation
Approaches: Conferences, publications, technical assistance,
training
Scope: International
Special projects: Transportation Assessment for Asia, Multilater-
al Development Bank Assessment of Energy Loans
Periodicals: *E Notes* (newsletter)

**International Research Center for Energy & Economic
Development**
Campus Box 263
University of Colorado
Boulder, CO 80309-0263
Phone: 303-492-7667   Fax: 303-442-5042
Dorothea El Mallakh, Director
Purpose: To examine the link between energy and development,
including issues of conservation, finance and management,
and energy resources.
Founded: 1973
FYR: 1990
Revenue: Not available
Expenditures: Not available
Staff: 4
Topics: Conservation, development, energy resources
Approaches: Conferences, publications, research
Scope: International
Special projects: Energy, Economics, and Environment
Conference

Periodicals: *Journal of Energy and Development*
Books: Yes
Reports: Yes

Northeast-Midwest Institute
218 D Street, SE
Washington, DC 20003
Phone: 202-544-5200   Fax: 202-544-0043
Dick Munson, Executive Director
Purpose: To ensure the future economic vitality of those states that historically have formed the nation's industrial heartland.
Founded: 1977
FYR: 1990
Revenue: [$1,100,500]
Expenditures: [$1,100,500]
Staff: 15
Topics: Development, energy, human resources
Approaches: Conferences, policy, publications, research
Scope: Regional (midwestern and northeastern United States)
Special projects: Abandoned Factory Toxics Cleanup
Periodicals: *Northeast-Midwest Economic Review* (newsletter)
Books: Yes
Reports: Yes

Rocky Mountain Institute
1739 Snowmass Creek Road
Old Snowmass, CO 81654-9199
Phone: 303-927-3851   Fax: 303-927-4178
L. Hunter Lovins, President
Purpose: With a primary focus on energy, RMI uses an imaginative and multi-dimensional approach in its efforts to foster the efficient and sustainable use of resources worldwide.
Founded: 1982
FYR: 1990
Revenue: [$1,100,000]
Expenditures: [$1,000,000]
Staff: 39

Topics: Energy efficiency, energy policy, security, sustainable agriculture, water use
Approaches: Advocacy, conferences, education, policy, publications, research
Scope: International
Periodicals: *Rocky Mountain Institute* (newsletter)
Reports: Yes

Union of Concerned Scientists
26 Church Street
Cambridge, MA 02238
Phone: 617-547-5552   Fax: 617-864-9405
Howard C. Ris, Jr., Executive Director
Purpose: To provide a forum for scientists' views on the social impact of technology, especially with regard to energy and arms.
Founded: 1969
FYR: 1990
Revenue: $3,296,038
Expenditures: $3,261,886
1990 membership: 100,000
Staff: 30
Topics: Energy efficiency, energy policy, military issues, nuclear issues, security, transportation
Approaches: Advocacy, conferences, education, lobbying, policy, publications, research
Scope: National
Periodicals: *Nucleus* (newsletter)
Books: Yes
Reports: Yes

❑ *Foundation Funding*

In 1990, about 8 percent of the dollars awarded by U.S. independent and community foundations for environmental programs went for energy projects.

☐ **ENVIRONMENTAL GRANT-MAKING FOUNDATIONS:** ☐
FUNDING FOR ENERGY PROJECTS 1990

Rank	Foundation	Number of Grants	Dollars Awarded
1	The Pew Charitable Trusts	10	6,969,000
2	The New York Community Trust	1	3,973,621
3	The Rockefeller Foundation	12	2,886,000
4	The Chicago Community Trust	1	1,868,000
5	John D. and Catherine T. MacArthur Foundation	5	883,500
6	Changing Horizons Charitable Trust	23	810,000
7	Joyce Mertz-Gilmore Foundation	12	700,000
8	Surdna Foundation, Inc.	7	690,000
9	The Joyce Foundation	8	432,039
10	Charles Stewart Mott Foundation	7	365,000

5

Climate And Atmosphere

DURING THE PAST SEVERAL YEARS, we've seen mounting evidence that human activities are changing our global climate. Of the changes that scientists perceive or predict, global warming and stratospheric ozone depletion seem most worrisome.

GLOBAL WARMING

During the very hot summer of 1988, we began to hear about global warming. Predictions that three years ago seemed outlandish are now generally accepted as true. According to the global warming hypothesis:

- Through industry, deforestation, and other activities, humans are spewing forth enormous amounts of carbon dioxide and other waste gases.

- These gases are accumulating in the atmosphere. They allow sunlight to pass through and onto the Earth but block the Earth's heat as it radiates back toward space.

- Although we do not know for certain what the end result of these increasing "greenhouse gases" will be, most scientists think they will create a warming trend on the surface of the Earth.

Greenhouse Gases

Carbon dioxide, methane, chlorofluorocarbons (CFCs), and nitrous oxide are the main greenhouse gases. Carbon dioxide accounts for 49 percent of world greenhouse gases. Its concentration in the atmosphere has increased by 25 percent since the pre-industrial era.

Greenhouse Gases:
Contribution to the Greenhouse Effect

Carbon dioxide	49%
Methane	18%
Chlorofluorocarbons	14%
Nitrous oxides	6%
Other	13%

Energy consumption, particularly through combustion of fossil fuels, is responsible for about 56 percent of greenhouse gas emissions. Tropical deforestation also plays an important role. Trees naturally act as a "sink" for carbon dioxide. When cut or burned, they can no longer absorb gases from the air, and they themselves give off carbon dioxide as they decompose.

Emissions of carbon dioxide have quadrupled since 1950. In the late 1980s, atmospheric concentrations of carbon dioxide increased at a rate of .05 percent each year. But thus far in the 1990s, the picture has changed slightly. According the World-watch Institute, global emissions in 1990 were 5.803 billion tons, down from 5.813 billion tons emitted during 1989. The decrease is attributed to the economic collapse of Eastern Europe, which is heavily dependent on coal. It illustrates that global carbon dioxide emissions could be reduced through the use of more efficient fuels and industrial processes. However, the Department of Energy estimates that releases from human activity need to be reduced by at least 80 percent before atmospheric carbon dioxide concentrations will stop increasing.

The Effect of Global Warming

Warming is expected to be as great as 3° to 8°F over the next century. Variation of a few degrees does not seem very important, but, in fact, it is. Historically, global temperature changes of about 8°F triggered the ice ages. The effect of the projected temperature change could thus be devastating. Warming is expected to cause:

- Altered patterns of climate and weather, bringing floods, droughts, fierce tropical storms, and hotter temperatures.

- Inundation of coastal regions where most of the world's population lives. Coastal wetlands would also be washed away, resulting in a loss of marine life.

- Rapid shifts in climate zones that would destroy ecosystems, sending many species to extinction. Farmers would have to change their crops or farming practices or move themselves poleward to continue farming.

The Evidence

The hottest year on record was 1990, and six of the seven warmest years ever recorded have occurred since 1980. Still, it's not entirely clear that warming has, in fact, begun.

Also, the evidence that warming will occur is not incontrovertible. A complex web of feedbacks links the atmosphere, oceans, and other Earth systems. Some scientists believe that these feedbacks will compensate for the accumulation of greenhouse gases and prevent warming (or even precipitate a cooling trend).

Policy

A number of international meetings on warming have been held since the first in 1985. For the most part, the United States has taken a cautious posture, arguing that there is insufficient evidence for action.

Recently, the position of the Bush administration appeared to mellow slightly. At the February 1991 meeting of the U.N. Intergovernmental Negotiating Committee, the United States agreed with all other parties:

- To work on a comprehensive approach to warming.

- To work toward a convention that includes controls on greenhouse gas emissions, transfer of technology and financial resources to developing countries, and international scientific and technological cooperation.

- To set up a special fund to subsidize the participation of delegates from developing countries.

The United States asserted that it was reducing greenhouse emissions. But each of the measures mentioned comes from legislation or programs already in place. These include:

- CFC elimination under the Montreal Protocol;

- Reductions in tropospheric ozone expected from the 1990 Clean Air Act Amendments;

- Proposals for reforestation in the United States included in the administration's 1992 budget proposal; and

- Energy efficiency and other provisions of the National Energy Strategy.

The strategy by the world's biggest greenhouse gas producer thus includes neither emission targets nor new policy responses. It will not solve the warming problem and it will not set much of an example for the rest of the world.

A much more aggressive approach to global warming is needed that includes:

1. *A plan to stabilize global emissions.* This can occur by reducing energy demand altogether, shifting from fossil fuels to renewables, or using less carbon-intensive fossil fuels.

   • Reducing energy demand is the best option, but is not likely to happen on a global scale with population increasing so rapidly. In the United States, the energy hog of the world, we can do a great deal in this regard as we did in the 1970s.

   • Opponents of a total shift to renewables in the United States by the year 2010 estimate it would cost from $800 billion to $3.6 trillion. Advocates for the shift argue that it would actually result in cost savings.

   • Fossil fuel switching is useful in the short term. A switch from coal to natural gas would, for instance, produce half as much carbon dioxide. A switch from coal to oil or oil to gas would produce roughly 30 percent less carbon dioxide.

2. *A plan to get the cooperation of the developing countries.* Energy use in many developing countries is already growing at twice the global rate: It may reach four times the 1980 energy use rate by the year 2000. Rapid development, not climate conservation, is the goal of these countries. In the case of China and India, the energy for development is slated to come from indigenous coal reserves. The coal reserves in China are enormous.

Cooperation of these countries will doubtless require:

- Financial incentives; and

- An international treaty or convention that is strong but flexible enough to accommodate political interests and new scientific findings as they develop.

3. *Some preparation for adaptation to warming.* In April 1991, the National Academy of Sciences released a report recommending a moderate mix of policy responses to the warming threat. It did not advocate aggressive measures to reduce demand such as a cap on greenhouse gas emissions or energy taxes. It did recommend research on adaptation to warming. Many environmentalists were disappointed.

OZONE DEPLETION

Ozone is most highly concentrated in the upper atmosphere, where it blocks harmful ultraviolet rays from reaching the Earth. Without the stratospheric ozone shield, there could be no life on Earth.

We have learned in the last few years that the synthetic compounds called chlorofluorocarbons (CFCs) are harming the ozone layer. CFCs are found in a number of useful products and manufacturing processes, particularly in refrigerants and in the propellants used to manufacture rigid foams. Chlorine, released when CFCs break down, drifts gradually to the stratosphere where it interacts with ozone molecules and destroys them.

Losses in the stratospheric ozone layer have been greatest above Antarctica. Scientists recorded a 60 percent loss of ozone in the Antarctic during the seasonal ozone "hole" of 1987. The 1988 hole was smaller, but those of 1989 and 1990 were larger again. In 1990, the hole persisted longer than in any of the previous years. Since 1959, Antarctic ozone has declined overall a total of 5 percent.

In 1990 scientists were astonished to learn from the National Aeronautics and Space Administration (NASA) Total Ozone Monitoring System (TOMS) that there has been a considerable loss in total ozone over northern latitudes as well as southern. Altogether, a 3 percent loss has been measured over eleven years.

In 1991, NASA launched the Airborne Arctic Stratospheric Expedition (AASE II) to investigate the Arctic polar stratosphere over the complete annual lifetime of the northern hemisphere polar vortex.

Effects

Increased exposure to ultraviolet radiation is expected to have a serious impact on plants and animals. It will likely lead to more skin cancers, cataracts, and immune suppression in humans and other animals. Plankton, the base of the marine food chain, are particularly sensitive to ultraviolet radiation. During the 1988 ozone hole over Antarctica, phytoplankton photosynthesis declined by 15 to 20 percent. A loss in plankton will have far-reaching consequences throughout the marine food web, affecting fish stocks, birds, and marine mammals. Many human food crops appear vulnerable to damage from ultraviolet radiation as well.

Policy

In 1978 the EPA banned production of most aerosols containing CFCs. Manufacturers are now working on alternative chemicals to replace CFCs in refrigeration systems and manufacturing. Yet even if all CFC production ceases today, the problem will continue for decades. CFCs are extremely stable chemicals that take as much as a century to break down.

Most CFCs are manufactured in the United States, but their release is occurring worldwide. There are already 150 million cars on the road that use CFCs in their air conditioners; China is said to have several hundred thousand CFC-containing refrigerators on order. This is indeed a global issue, demanding global solutions. Progress has been as follows:

- In 1987, a landmark international agreement on CFCs was reached. The Montreal Protocol on Substances that Deplete the Ozone Layer requires participating countries to cut CFC consumption 50 percent by 1998 and to freeze consumption of halons (related compounds that also destroy CFCs) by 1992. As of January 1992, 72 countries had signed the Protocol. Yet even with full compliance, atmospheric chlorine is expected to triple by the year 2075.

- Several international meetings have been held since the Montreal Protocol to consider strengthening its provisions. Until February 1992, the United States has opposed the aggressive controls on CFC production suggested by many European nations and by Britain.

- In July 1992, the fourth meeting of the Contracting Parties will convene.

On April 16, 1991, Dr. Robert T. Watson of NASA testified before the Senate Subcommittee on Science, Technology and Space:

> While the cause of the observed ozone depletion has not been unequivocally identified, the ozone changes coupled with other atmospheric data are strongly suggestive of a chlorine-induced effect. If, indeed, the observed decrease in mid-latitude ozone is caused by anthropogenic chlorine emissions, and to a lesser extent bromine emissions, then it is clear that the amount of ozone will continue to decrease over the next decade or so as the stratospheric abundances of chlorine and bromine increase in response to the continued emissions of CFCs, methylchloroform, carbon tetrachloride, halons, and other halogenated substances.

- On December 3, 1991, environmentalists submitted a petition to the EPA suggesting an accelerated schedule for ozone-depleting substances. The petition called for a 60 percent reduction in CFCs (and methyl bromine) by 1992, with a complete halt in production by 1993. The EPA has said that those targets would be hard to reach, but that moving phase-out date for CFCs and halons from 2000 to 1995 or 1997 would be feasible.

- On December 17, 1991, Dr. Watson testified again—this time before the Senate Governmental Affairs Ad Hoc Subcommittee on Consumer and Environmental Affairs. Predicting that the Antarctic ozone hole may still exist in 2050 or 2100, he too urged an accelerated schedule for CFC phaseout. He also urged the United States to consider regulations on new substitute gases for the ozone depleters. Although these may represent "a considerable step forward," many of these still contain chlorine and may also have an effect on global warming. Watson suggested that such gases are thus only "pragmatic substitutes for the short term."

RESOURCES

☙ Books and Reports

Assessing Carbon Emissions Control Strategies: A Carbon Tax or a Gasoline Tax? ACEEE Policy Paper No. 3. W. U. Chandler, and A. K. Nicholls. Washington, DC: American Council for an Energy-Efficient Economy. 1990, 53 pp.

Atmospheric Carbon Dioxide and the Greenhouse Effect. Washington, DC: Department of Energy. 1989, 36 pp.

The Challenge of Global Warming. Dean Edwin Abrahamson, editor. Natural Resources Defense Council. Washington, DC: Island Press. 1989, 356 pp.

Changes by Degrees: Steps to Reduce Greenhouse Gases. OTA-0-482. U.S. Congress, Office of Technology Assessment. Washington, DC: Government Printing Office. 1991, 370 pp.

Climate Change: The IPCC Response Strategies. Intergovernmental Panel on Climate Change. Washington, DC: Island Press, 1991, 272 pp.

Escaping the Heat Trap: Probing the Prospects for a Stable Environment. Irving Mintzer and William R. Moomaw. Washington, DC: World Resources Institute. April 1992, 104 pp.

Global Climate Change and Our Common Future: Papers from a Forum. National Research Council. Washington, DC: National Academy Press. 1989, 227 pp.

Global Warming. Stephen H. Schneider. San Francisco: Sierra Club Books. 1989, 317 pp.

The Greenhouse Effect: Investment Implications and Opportunities. Douglas G. Cogan, editor. Washington, DC: Investment Responsibility Research Center. 1989, 158 pp.

The Greenhouse Trap. Francesca Lyman. World Resources Institute. Boston: Beacon Press.1990, 190 pp.

Greenhouse Warming: Negotiating a Global Regime. Jessica Tuchman Mathews, editor. Washington, DC: World Resources Institute. 1991, 80 pp.

The Heat Is On: America's CO_2 Polluters. Washington, DC: Citizen Action. 1990, 40 pp.

The Heated Debate: Greenhouse Predictions versus Climate Reality. Robert C. Balling, Jr. Introduction by Aaron Wildavsky. San Francisco: Pacific Research Institute for Public Policy. Spring 1992, 250 pp.

Keeping It Green: Tropical Forestry and the Mitigation of Global Warming. Mark C. Trexler. Washington, DC: World Resources Institute. 1991, 75 pp.

Minding the Carbon Store: Weighing U.S. Forestry Strategies to Slow Global Warming. Mark C. Trexler. Washington, DC: World Resources Institute. 1991, 75 pp.

Ominous Future: Under the Ozone Hole: Assessing Biological Impacts in Antarctica. Mary A. Voytek. Washington, DC: Environmental Defense Fund. 1989, 69 pp.

Ozone Depletion, Greenhouse Gases, and Climate Change. National Research Council. Washington, DC: National Academy Press. 1989, 122 pp.

The Ozone Layer. Nairobi: United Nations Environment Programme. 1989, 35 pp.

Policy Implications of Greenhouse Warming. Committee on Science, Engineering and Public Policy. Washington, DC: National Academy Press. 1991, 127 pp.

Present State of Knowledge of the Upper Atmosphere 1990: An Assessment Report. R. T. Watson, M. J. Kurylo, M. J. Prather, and F. M. Ormond. NASA Reference Publication 1242. Washington, DC: NASA Office of Space Science and Applications. 1990, 136 pp.

Protecting Life on Earth: Steps to Save the Ozone Layer. Worldwatch Paper 87. Cynthea Pollock Shea. Washington, DC: Worldwatch Institute. December 1988, 46 pp.

Responding to Changes in Sea Level: Engineering Implications. National Research Council. Washington, DC: National Academy Press. 1987, 140 pp.

Slowing Global Warming: A Worldwide Strategy. Worldwatch Paper 91. Christopher Flavin. Washington, DC: Worldwatch Institute. October 1989, 94 pp.

Stones in a Glass House: CFCs and Ozone Depletion. Douglas G. Cogan. Washington, DC: Investor Responsibility Research Center. 1988, 147 pp.

Trends '90: A Compendium of Data on Global Change. Thomas A. Boden, Paul Kanciruk, and Michael P. Farrell. Oak Ridge, TN: Carbon Dioxide Information Analysis Center. August 1990, 257 pp.

✪ Periodicals

Atmosphere
Friends of the Earth
218 D Street, SE
Washington, DC 20003
Phone: 202-544-2600   Fax: 202-543-4710
Liz Cook, Editor

Type: Newsletter
Frequency: Quarterly
Length: 8 pp.
Subscription fee: $15
Topics: Ozone depletion, treaties
Coverage: Activism, business/industry, organization activities, policy, research
Audience: Citizens
Scope: International
Comment: An accessible newsbrief about stratospheric ozone depletion.

CDIAC Communications

Carbon Dioxide Information Analysis Center
Oak Ridge National Laboratory
P.O. Box 2008
Oak Ridge, TN 37831-6335
Phone: 615-574-0390   Fax: 615-574-2232
David Fowler, Managing Editor
Type: Newsletter
Frequency: Semiannual
Length: 16 pp.
Subscription fee: Free
Topics: Carbon emissions, climate change, global warming, greenhouse effect
Coverage: Book reviews, conference proceedings, research
Audience: Professional/academic
Scope: Global
Comment: A superb publication on carbon dioxide and climate change from the Oak Ridge National Laboratory.

Climate Alert

The Climate Institute
316 Pennsylvania Avenue, SE
Washington, DC 20003
Phone: 202-547-0104   Fax: 202-547-0111
Nancy Wilson, Editor
Type: Newsletter
Frequency: 10 issues per year

Length: 8 to 16 pp.
Subscription fee: $95
Topics: Climate change, global warming, ozone depletion
Coverage: Policy, research
Scope: Global
Audience: Government, professional/academic
Comment: Readable updates on climate change.

Global Climate Change Digest
Elsevier Science Publishing Co., Inc.
655 Avenue of the Americas
New York, NY 10010
Phone: 212-989-5800   Fax: 212-663-3990
Dr. Robert W. Pratt, Editor
Type: Newsletter
Frequency: Monthly
Length: 12 pp.
Subscription fee: $190
Topics: Global warming, ozone depletion, treaties
Coverage: Book reviews, business/industry, organization activities, research
Audience: Professional/academic
Scope: Global
Comment: One of the best available summaries on climate change science and policy.

❖ Organizations

The Carbon Dioxide Information Analysis Center
MS-6335, Building 1000
Oak Ridge National Laboratory
P.O. Box 2008
Oak Ridge, TN 37831-6335
Phone: 615-574-0390   Fax: 615-574-2232
Paul Kanciruk, Director
Purpose: To collect, verify, and distribute data related to carbon dioxide and global climate change.
Founded: 1982

FYR: 1990
Revenue: [$1.3 million]
Expenditures: [$1.3 million]
Staff: 12
Topics: Carbon dioxide, climate change, global warming, inventories
Approaches: Conferences, education, funding, publications, research
Scope: Global
Special projects: Global Climate Database
Periodicals: *CDIAC Communications* (newsletter)
Reports: Yes

Center for Global Change
University of Maryland at College Park
The Executive Building, Suite 401
7100 Baltimore Avenue
College Park, MD 20740
Phone: 301-403-4165   Fax: 301-403-4292
Allan Miller, Executive Director
Purpose: To conduct interdisciplinary research on issues of environmental quality and their relationship to energy use and economic growth.
Founded: 1989
FYR: 1990
Revenue: $984,126
Expenditures: $984,126
Staff: 15
Topics: Fossil fuels, global warming, renewable energy, utilities
Approaches: Conferences, education, policy, publications, research
Scope: Global
Special projects: Sea Level Rise, Global Journal Directory, Renewable Energy Technologies, Southern California Edison Greenhouse Gas Reduction Project
Reports: Yes

The Climate Institute
316 Pennsylvania Avenue, SE

Washington, DC 20003
Phone: 202-547-0104   Fax: 202-547-0111
John Topping, Jr., President
Purpose: To act as a worldwide bridge between scientists, governments, and private decision makers on greenhouse warming and stratospheric ozone depletion.
Founded: July 1986
FYR: 1990
Revenue: [$488,000]
Expenditures: [$568,000]
1990 membership: 6,500
Staff: 10+
Topics: Developing countries, global warming, ozone depletion
Approaches: Conferences, education, funding, grassroots organizing, policy, publications, research
Scope: Global
Special projects: Greenhouse Effects Slide Project, Ministerial Briefings Project, Global Climate Change Conference
Periodicals: *Climate Alert* (newsletter)
Books: Yes
Reports: Yes

National Center for Atmospheric Research
P.O. Box 3000
Boulder, CO 80307
Phone: 303-497-1000
Robert Serafin, Director
Purpose: Funded mainly by government, this center has scientists from fourteen universities who share equipment and collaborate on basic research projects on global climate change.
Founded: 1960
FYR: 1991
Revenue: [$67,800,000]
Expenditures: [$67,800,000]
Staff: 646
Topics: Climate change, global warming
Approaches: Conferences, education, funding, publications, research
Reports: Yes

The Woods Hole Research Center
13 Church Street
Woods Hole, MA 02543
Phone: 508-540-9900   Fax: 508-540-9700
George Woodwell, Director
Purpose: To study how the Earth's ecosystems work and how humans are changing those ecosystems.
Founded: 1985
FYR: 1990
Revenue: [$2,100,000]
Expenditures: [$2,100,000]
Staff: 23
Topics: Biota, climate change, ecosystems, forests, global warming, rain forest destruction
Approaches: Advocacy, conferences, education, policy, publications, research
Scope: Global
Special projects: The interaction between global warming and forest ecosystems
Reports: Yes

❏ Foundation Funding

In 1990, about 3 percent of the dollars contributed for environmental programs by U.S. independent and community foundations went for projects dealing with climate and atmosphere.

❏   ENVIRONMENTAL GRANT-MAKING FOUNDATIONS: ❏
FUNDING FOR CLIMATE PROJECTS 1990

Rank	Foundation	Number of Grants	Dollars Awarded
1	John D. and Catherine T. MacArthur Foundation	4	940,783
2	Public Welfare Foundation, Inc.	5	890,000
3	The Ford Foundation	8	861,589
4	W. Alton Jones Foundation, Inc.	7	670,000
5	Great Lakes Protection Fund	3	507,294
6	Joyce Mertz-Gilmore Foundation	12	407,000
7	The Rockefeller Foundation	5	386,050
8	Pew Scholars Program in Conservation and the Environment	2	300,000
9	The James Irving Foundation	1	250,000
10	The Joyce Foundation	3	230,000

6

Biodiversity

The human species came into being at the time of greatest biological diversity in the history of the earth. Today as human populations expand and alter the natural environment, they are reducing biological diversity to its lowest level since the end of the Mesozoic era, 65 million years ago. The ultimate consequences of this biological collision are beyond calculation and certain to be harmful.

EDWARD O. WILSON, 1989

BIODIVERSITY DESCRIBES THE VARIety of plants and animals that live on Earth. Scientists know surprisingly little about the range of biodiversity; they do not even know to the nearest order of magnitude how many species there are (current estimates vary from 5 million to 30 million or more). But they do know that biodiversity is essential to life on Earth.

About 70 percent of the world's plant and animal species live in the humid tropics, mainly in the rain forests that cover about 7 percent of the Earth's surface. The countries with the greatest numbers of species are Brazil, Colombia, and Indonesia. These three, together with ten other priority countries (Australia, China, Ecuador, India, Malaysia, Madagascar, Mexico, Peru, Venezuela, and Zaire), are thought to contain more than 60 percent of the world's species.

Biological diversity occurs on three levels: genetic, species, and ecosystem. On the most detailed level, genetic diversity includes the factors that enable individual organisms to differ from one other and to adapt to environmental change. Species diversity comprises large classes of organisms. Finally and most broadly, ecosystem diversity describes the species groups that live together in various habitats.

Altogether, biodiversity benefits the human species in the following ways:

POTENTIAL PRODUCTS. A large gene pool is needed for:

- *Food.* At least 75,000 wild species have edible parts. Wild species provide a genetic reservoir from which we can draw to improve existing crop strains or regenerate populations affected by disease.

- *Medicines.* About half the prescription and nonprescription drugs used in the world and 25 percent of those used in the United States have active ingredients from wild plants. Annual sales of drugs based on natural chemicals are $20 billion to $40 billion. These drugs are used to treat a variety of diseases including heart disease and cancer, both major causes of morbidity and mortality in modern industrial society. Scientists have identified at least 1,400 plant species that have anti-cancer properties. They're now looking at plants in the hopes of discovering a cure for AIDS.

  An example of a plant with medical value is the yew found in the ancient forests of the Pacific northwest. Its bark is used to make Taxol, a drug recently found useful in the treatment of breast cancer. The survival of this plant, like the others in the ancient forest, is threatened by clear cutting, the logging method of choice in the logging industry.

- *Other products.* Fibers, glue, soap, leather, down, wool, and petroleum substitutes are derived from natural sources.

ECOSYSTEM SERVICES. Diverse natural ecosystems of plants, animals, and microbes moderate our climate, produce the oxygen we breathe, cleanse the water we drink, recycle nutrients needed for agriculture, and degrade waste.

AESTHETIC VALUES. Diverse habitats and the plants and animals they house are a source of beauty and wonder for increasing numbers of people. In the United States, some 95 million people engage in outdoor recreation in wildlife areas every year. Another 54 million fish and 16 million hunt. Still others derive pleasure just from knowing that wildlife exists.

Revenue is a tangible byproduct of recreation. Americans spend $37 billion each year for their activities in wildlife areas. In the less developed countries, ecotourism is proving an important source of revenue. In Kenya, for example, tourism brought $300 million in 1985. It has been estimated that one male lion living for seven years in Kenya is worth $515,000 of tourist dollars. Killed for its skin, it would be worth only $1,000.

There is still another reason for preserving biodiversity. It has nothing to do with the various "services" these species provide; it is the fact that they are living things that cohabit the planet with us. Put another way, human beings are just one of millions of living organisms that share the Earth. There is an extremely persuasive argument that the other organisms have just as much right to survive and flourish as we. It is also true that diverse ecosystems and populations are more resilient than impoverished ones. They are better able to adapt to changes in climate or habitat, and they provide the gene pool necessary to continue the process of evolution in the future.

We are in the midst of a biodiversity crisis. Humans are destroying species at an accelerating rate. We may be extinguishing 4,000 to 6,000 species a year, many of which have never been described. We are, for the most part, killing off species inadvertently as we destroy their habitats. But humans are also deliberately snuffing out select species, such as the African elephant and certain populations of whales.

There are several possible approaches to this crisis. The first deals with genetic diversity, the second with species, and the third with habitat:

1. *Gene banks.* Scientists are now carefully preserving basic genetic material for certain kinds of wild and domesticated plants and animals. The American Minor Breeds Conservancy has recently set up such a bank to preserve rare strains of livestock. Private groups like "Seed Savers" do the same for plants. The U.S. Department of Agriculture operates a seed bank, but it is greatly underfunded.

2. *Legislation.* There is both a national law and an international convention designed to protect endangered and threatened species. In North America alone, as many as 500 species and subspecies of native plants and animals have become extinct since the first Europeans arrived. Even since the U.S. Endangered Species Act was enacted in 1973, seven listed species have been extinguished; several others are teetering on the brink. The official list of threatened and endangered species now includes more than 560 species; there are about 6,000 candidates for listing.

   The Endangered Species Act is due for reauthorization in 1992. Congressman Studds (D-MA) has introduced a bill that would broaden the law to deal with ecosystems instead of only single species. Other members of congress hope to weaken the law by requiring economic impact to be considered when listing a species.

   Like the Endangered Species Act, the Convention on International Trade in Endangered Species (CITES) works on a species-by-species basis. One hundred ten countries are now party to CITES. The Convention has been useful in the rescue of certain species, such as the leopard, and may help prevent the total demise of the African elephant through its 1989 total ban on trade in ivory.

   But in both the national and international arenas, the process of listing species is tortuous and highly political, as anyone knows who has followed the story of the spotted owl in the Pacific northwest. And since relatively few species even have names, such a listing process could never truly remedy the biodiversity problem.

3. *Zoos and botanical gardens.* Once grim, barred sites to view wildlife, zoos are now "arks" for the sequestration and breeding of rare and endangered animal species. Zoos now house over one-half million individual animals, but these represent only 900 of several thousand endangered and threatened species. Botanical gardens carry out a similar function for some of the 67,000 rare and endangered plants species that have been identified worldwide.

But many scientists think the species approach will inherently fail: We simply cannot do the job on a case-by-case basis. Not only are there too many species, but an inappropriate amount of attention seems to go to a few "charismatic" animal species that are big, smart, or cute and that people easily relate to. These may not be the most important species to worry about. And ultimately, even when attempting to preserve individual species, one is forced to consider the broader issue of habitat or ecosystem.

HABITAT. Species diversity has been fairly constant over the last 250 million years, with the exception of a few brief periods of accelerated extinction that occurred roughly every 26 million years. But over the last half century, human activities have had a devastating impact on the habitats of many species. Habitats, of course, exist all over the planet. But many scientists believe that the habitats of greatest concern are those that are home to the greatest numbers of species. These include ancient forests, ancient lakes, coastal wetlands, coral reefs, riparian lands, and tropical rain forests.

Tropical rain forests, for example, are believed to support 70 percent of the Earth's species. Tropical rain forests have already been reduced to about 55 percent of their original cover; they are currently being cut at a rate of some 100,000 square kilometers a year. At this rate, these forests will disappear totally within the next century, taking with them hundreds of thousands of species into extinction.

Human activities also threaten habitat in more subtle ways. If current predictions hold true, climate changes associated with global warming could prove disastrous for many species. Warming is likely to affect storm patterns and precipitation as well as temperature. As climatic zones march poleward at a rate greater than 100 kilometers per century, most wild species will not be able to keep pace or adapt fast enough to survive. Even the species potentially able to move will have a hard time of it, as they struggle to cross the numerous man-made impediments —cities, roads, and farms—that block their way.

A huge international effort is now under way to deal with the problem of habitat and ecosystem destruction. Among the strategies:

- *Mapping.* Conservation biologists are working to identify the hot-spot habitats that are both rich in species and in imminent danger of destruction. Classifying the world's species is a companion task. As part of this effort, The Nature Conservancy has developed a natural heritage database with information for species and habitats in each of the fifty states and a growing number of countries in Latin American and Asia.

- *Land preservation.* There are many efforts afoot to set aside lands rich in biodiversity. A key question: How big does a reserve have to be to protect its indigenous species? The World Wildlife Fund's Minimum Critical Size Project in Amazonia addresses that question. As general deforestation continues, large blocks of different sizes have been left so that scientists can measure the effect of habitat size on species survival.

  In the United States, 261 unique ecosystem types have been identified. About 40 percent of these are currently not represented in our national wilderness preservation system. And of those represented, not all may exist in large enough blocks to adequately protect their indigenous species. At present many of the reserves are not linked so that their species survive in a series of unconnected islands.

- *International debt reduction.* Species extinction is occurring fastest in the less developed countries. The biologically diverse nations of Asia, Africa, and Latin America have enormous population pressures, compounded by huge debts to industrial nations. With incentives to produce cash crops (to pay off their debt), many of these nations encourage their poor to settle and farm previously wild lands. In the process, habitats are destroyed.

Conservation International and other environmental organizations are working to find creative solutions to the debt problem that will give species-rich countries financial incentives to set aside sensitive lands. "Debt-for-nature swaps" is one idea that has been somewhat successful on a very small scale.

- *Ecotourism.* If the camera-laden tourists don't crush the habitats they visit, ecotourism is one way to encourage wildland preservation in the less developed countries.

- *Sustainable use.* Recent studies show that more income can be extracted from the sustained harvesting of natural products in the tropical forest than from clear-cutting for timber and agriculture. This should be our model as we seek to preserve other ecosystems.

All strategies on a genetic, species, and ecosystem level have a role in what has become an all-out battle to preserve biodiversity. For as the number of species dwindles, the Earth becomes a far less interesting—and a far less habitable—place.

RESOURCES

☙ Books and Reports

Animal Extinctions: What Everyone Should Know. R. J. Hoage, editor. Washington, DC: Smithsonian Institution Press. 1985, 192 pp.

Balancing on the Brink of Extinction: The Endangered Species Act and Lessons for the Future. Kathryn A. Kohm, editor. Washington, DC: Island Press. 1991, 316 pp.

Biodiversity. E. O. Wilson, editor. Washington, DC: National Academy Press. 1988, 521 pp.

Conservation Biology: The Science of Scarcity and Diversity. Michael E. Soule, editor. Sunderland, MA: Sinauer Associates, Inc. 1986, 584 pp.

Conserving Biological Diversity in Our National Forests. Washington, DC: The Wilderness Society. 1986, 116 pp.

The End of the Game. Peter Beard. San Francisco: Chronicle Books. 1988, no pagination.

Extinction: The Causes and Consequences of the Disappearance of Species. Paul and Anne Ehrlich. New York: Ballantine Books. 1981, 384 pp.

Investing in Biological Diversity: U.S. Research and Conservation Efforts in Developing Countries. Janet N. Abramovitz. Washington, DC: World Resources Institute. 1991, 100 pp.

Keeping Options Alive: The Scientific Basis for Conserving Biodiversity. Walter V. Reid and Kenton R. Miller. Washington, DC: World Resources Institute. October 1989, 128 pp.

The Last Extinction. Les Kaufman and Kenneth Mallory, editors. Cambridge, MA: MIT Press. 1987, 208 pp.

Last Animals at the Zoo: How Mass Extinction Can be Stopped. Colin Tudge. Washington, DC: Island Press. March 1992, 266 pp.

On the Brink of Extinction: Conserving the Diversity of Life. Edward C. Wolf. Washington, DC: Worldwatch Institute. June 1987, 54 pp.

The Preservation of Species: The Value of Biological Diversity. Bryan G. Norton, editor. Princeton, NJ: Princeton University Press. 1986, 305 pp.

The Primary Source: Tropical Forests and Our Future. Norman Myers. New York: W. W. Norton & Company. 1984, 399 pp.

Rain Forest in Your Kitchen: The Hidden Connection between Extinction and your Supermarket. Martin Teitel with a foreword by Jeremy Rifkin. Washington, DC: Island Press. May 1992, 120 pp.

The Sinking Ark. Norman Myers. New York: Pergamon Press. 1979, 307 pp.

Sustainable Harvest and Marketing of Rain Forest Products. Mark Plotkin and Lisa Famolare. Conservation International. Washington, DC: Island Press. June 1992, 320 pp.

Technologies to Maintain Biological Diversity. Washington, DC: Office of Technology Assessment. 1987, 334 pp.

❂ Periodicals

The Animals' Voice Magazine
Compassion for Animals Foundation, Inc.
3960 Landmark Street
Culver City, CA 90232
Phone: 213-204-2323   Fax: 213-204-2578
Laura A. Moretti, Editor-in-Chief
Type: Magazine
Frequency: Bimonthly
Length: 80 pp.
Subscription fee: $20
Topics: Animal health/welfare, animal rights, wildlife
Coverage: Activism, organization activities, research
Audience: Citizens
Scope: International
References: Yes
Advertising: Yes
Comment: A fine publication with compelling tales about humans' heartless treatment of other animals.

BioScience
American Institute of Biological Sciences, Inc.
730 11th Street, NW
Washington, DC 20001-4584
Phone: 202-628-1500   Fax: 202-628-1509
Julie Ann Miller, Editor
Type: Journal
Frequency: 11 issues per year
Length: 70 pp.

Subscription fee: $43
Topics: Biodiversity, biology, ecology
Coverage: Organization activities, policy, research
Audience: Educators, professional/academic
Scope: National
References: Yes
Advertising: Yes
Comment: Although frequently on the technical side, Bio-
    Science often contains pieces on ecology and conservation
    biology that are accessible to the nonscientist.

Defenders

Defenders of Wildlife
1244 19th Street, NW
Washington, DC 20036
Phone: 202-659-9510   Fax: 202-833-3349
James G. Deane, Editor
Type: Magazine
Frequency: Bimonthly
Length: 50 pp.
Subscription fee: $20, free with membership
Topics: Biodiversity, ecosystem restoration, endangered species,
    habitats, rivers/streams, wildlife
Coverage: Activism, environmental community, organization
    activities, policy, science
Audience: Citizens
Scope: National
Advertising: Yes
Comment: This magazine describes problems of biodiversity in
    a way that engages the citizen directly: for example, by show-
    ing how population pressures affect species survival in our
    national parks.

Dolphin Alert

Earth Island Institute
300 Broadway, Suite 28
San Francisco, CA 94133
Phone: 415-788-3666   Fax: 415-788-7324
David Phillips, Editor

Type: Newsletter
Frequency: Quarterly
Length: 8 pp.
Subscription fee: Free with membership
Topics: Endangered species, marine issues, marine mammals
Coverage: Activism, organization activities
Audience: Citizens, environmental organizations
Scope: International

Endangered Species Technical Bulletin
United States Fish and Wildlife Service
440-ARLSQ
Department of the Interior
1849 C Street NW
Washington, DC 20240
Phone: 703-358-2166   Fax: 703-921-2232
Michael Bender, Editor
Type: Newsletter
Frequency: Monthly
Length: 12 pp.
Subscription fee: Free
Topics: Biodiversity, endangered species, wildlife
Coverage: Legislation, organization activities, research
Audience: Environmental organizations, professional/academic
Scope: National
Comment: Available to government agencies, this official sum-
    mary of what's happening on the endangered species front
    is of interest to citizens as well.

Endangered Species Update
University of Michigan, School of Natural Resources
Ann Arbor, MI 48109
Phone: 313-763-3243   Fax: 313-936-2195
Suzanne Jones, Editor
Type: Newsletter
Frequency: 10 issues per year
Length: 8 pp.
Subscription fee: $23
Topics: Biodiversity, endangered species

Coverage: Activism, environmental community, legislation, organization activities, research
Audience: Citizens, environmental organizations, government, professional/academic
Scope: National
Comment: Includes articles on species protection and a reprint of the latest *USFWS Endangered Species Technical Bulletin* (see above).

Focus
World Wildlife Fund
1250 24th Street, NW, Suite 500
Washington, DC 20037
Phone: 202-293-4800   Fax: 202-293-9211
Pamela S. Cubberly, Editor
Type: Newsletter
Frequency: Bimonthly
Length: 10 pp.
Subscription fee: Free with membership
Topics: Endangered species, wildlife conservation
Coverage: Activism, book reviews, organization activities, research
Audience: Citizens
Scope: International
Comment: News about World Wildlife Fund's widening array of conservation efforts, from an innovative "preventive" trust fund for Bhutan to remediation of the Zambian poaching problem.

International Wildlife
National Wildlife Federation
8925 Leesburg Pike NW
Vienna, VA 22184
Phone: 202-872-8840   Fax: 202-466-9042
Bob Strohm, Editor-in-Chief
Type: Magazine
Frequency: Bimonthly
Length: 50 pp.
Subscription fee: $15; free to international members and world members

Topics: Conservation, endangered species, wildlife
Coverage: Activism, organization activities, policy, research
Audience: Citizens
Scope: International
Comment: Endangered species are the theme for this magazine, which includes articles and photographs about science, history, and culture.

National Wildlife

National Wildlife Federation, Headquarters
8925 Leesburg Pike
Vienna, VA 22184
Phone: 202-797-6800   Fax: 202-442-7332
Mark Wexler, Editor
Type: Magazine
Frequency: Bimonthly
Length: 60 pp.
Subscription fee: $16; free to national members and world members
Topics: Biodiversity, endangered species, habitats, illegal wildlife trade, wildlife
Coverage: Business/industry, organization activities, research
Audience: Citizens
Scope: National
Comment: One of the best environmental "overview" magazines, *National Wildlife* has a fine layout and gorgeous illustrations and covers a wide range of topics. Of particular note is its annual "Environmental Quality Index" that assesses U.S. progress (or lack thereof) in several natural resource areas.

RARE Center News

RARE Center for Tropical Bird Conservation
1529 Walnut Street
Philadelphia, PA 19102
Phone: 215-568-0420   Fax: 215-568-0516
John Guarnaccia, Executive Director
Type: Newsletter
Frequency: Semiannual
Length: 5 pp.

Subscription fee: Free with membership
Topics: Birds, tropical conservation
Coverage: Book reviews, organization activities, policy, research
Audience: Citizens
Scope: International, with a geographic focus on the tropics
Comment: Documents the RARE Center's activities in tropical
    bird conservation in the Caribbean and Latin America

TRAFFIC USA
World Wildlife Fund
1250 24th Street, NW, Suite 500
Washington, DC 20037
Phone: 202-293-4800   Fax: 202-293-9211
Andrea L. Gaski, Managing Editor
Type: Newsletter
Frequency: Quarterly
Length: 24 pp.
Subscription fee: Free
Topics: Endangered species, illegal wildlife trade
Coverage: Book reviews, legislation, organization activities,
    policy, research
Audience: Citizens, professional/academic
Scope: International
Comment: This newsletter covers international trade in wildlife
    and wildlife products with in-depth reports, updates on the
    Convention for International Trade in Endangered Species
    (CITES), and newsbriefs. A recent issue included articles on
    bears, cacti, herbs, ivory, jaguars, orchids, parrots, timber,
    and turtles.

Tropicus
Conservation International
1015 18th Street, NW, Suite 1000
Washington, DC 20036
Phone: 202-429-5660   Fax: 202-887-5188
Edward C. Wolf, Editor

Type: Newsletter
Frequency: Quarterly
Length: 12 pp.
Subscription fee: Free with membership
Topics: Conservation, debt-for-nature swaps, ecosystems, endangered species, ethology, rain forests, sustainable development
Coverage: Book reviews, organization activities, policy, research
Audience: Citizens, environmental organizations
Scope: International
Comment: This quarterly newsletter reports on conservation efforts in tropical regions around the world, from wildlife in Botswana to ecosystem conservation in Japan and ethnobotany in Amazonia.

Wildlife Conservation
New York Zoological Society
185th Street and Southern Boulevard
Bronx, NY 10460
Phone: 212-220-5121   Fax: 212-584-2625
Joan Downs, Editor-in-Chief
Type: Magazine
Frequency: Bimonthly
Length: 90 pp.
Subscription fee: $13.95
Topics: Climate change, conservation, forests, genetic diversity, habitats, wildlife, zoos
Coverage: Activism, policy, research
Audience: Citizens
Scope: International
References: Yes
Advertising: Yes
Comments: An excellent publication about the human impact on habitat and species. Recent articles described what acid precipitation is doing to wildlife, how the "tame" wild elephant can't survive, and how developers threaten the Texas warbler.

❖ Organizations

American Association of Zoological Parks and Aquariums
Oglebay Park
Wheeling, WV 26003-1698
Phone: 304-242-2160   Fax: 304-242-2283
Robert O. Wagner, Executive Director
Purpose: A professional society, the AAZPA works to advance the
    role of zoological parks and aquariums in conservation, ed-
    ucation, scientific studies, and recreation.
Founded: 1924
FYR: 1990
Revenue: $1,130,150
Expenditures: $1,013,600
1990 membership: 5,800
Change from 1989: +5%
Staff: 18
Chapters: 2
Affiliates: International Union for the Conservation of Nature
    and Natural Resources (IUCN)
Topics: Biodiversity, endangered species, zoos/aquariums
Approaches: Conferences, education, funding, policy, publica-
    tions, research
Scope: International
Periodicals: *Communique* (newsletter)
Books: Yes
Reports: Yes

American Minor Breeds Conservancy
P.O. Box 477
Pittsboro, NC 27312
Phone: 919-542-5704
Donald Bixby, Executive Director
Purpose: To conserve and promote minor breeds of North
    American livestock. Minor breeds represent genetic diversity
    to meet the needs of the future.
Founded: 1977
FYR: 1991
Revenue: [$170,000]

Expenditures: [$170,000]
1990 membership: 3,600
Staff: 5
Affiliates: Rare Breeds International
Topics: Genetic diversity, livestock
Approaches: Advocacy, conferences, direct action, education, funding, grassroots organizing, policy, publications, research
Scope: International
Special projects: Exhibit of American Livestock Breeding Art, Rare Breeds Semen Bank, Sustainable Agriculture Policy Development
Periodicals: *AMBC News* (newsletter)
Books: Yes
Reports: Yes

Center for Plant Conservation
Missouri Botanical Garden
St. Louis, MO 63166
Phone: 314-577-9450   Fax: 314-664-0465
Donald A. Falk, Director
Purpose: Recently relocated from Boston to join the Missouri Botanical Garden, the Center works to conserve and preserve endangered plant species from around the world.
Founded: 1984
FYR: 1990
Revenue: $1,032,793
Expenditures: $751,753
Staff: 12
Affiliates: Missouri Botanical Garden
Topics: Endangered species, plant conservation
Approaches: Advocacy, conferences, funding, publications, research
Scope: National
Periodicals: *Plant Conservation* (newsletter)

Consultative Group on Biological Diversity
1290 Avenue of the Americas
New York, NY 10104
Phone: 212-373-4200   Fax: 212-315-0996

Theodore Smith, Executive Director
Purpose: This group, originally funded by the U.S. Agency for International Development (U.S. AID), is a consortium designed to encourage foundation activity in the field of natural resource conservation. CGBD now has about forty members with combined assets of some $15 billion. Grants from members have supported a wide range of activities, including debt-for-nature swaps, tropical plant research, a conference on the effect of climate change on biodiversity, and development of a handbook for national environmental accounting.
Founded: 1988
FYR: 1990
Revenue: Not available
Expenditures: Not available
Staff: 3
Topics: Ancient forests, biodiversity, the commons, developing countries, economic policy, marine issues, tropical forests
Approaches: Conferences, education, research
Scope: International
Special projects: Ancient Forests, Asian Biodiversity, Marine Biodiversity
Reports: Yes

Defenders of Wildlife
1244 19th Street, NW
Washington, DC 20036
Phone: 202-659-9510   Fax: 202-833-3349
Rodger Schlickeisen, President
Purpose: Working through advocacy and education to protect endangered wildlife and to preserve biodiversity and habitat.
Founded: 1947
FYR: 1990
Revenue: $6,521,597
Expenditures: $4,290,588
Staff: 35
Topics: Habitats, wildlife
Approaches: Advocacy, conferences, dispute resolution, education, litigation, lobbying, policy, publications, research

Scope: National
Special projects: Ban on importation of tropical birds, Florida
    Panther Restoration Project, Mexican Wolf Restoration Pro-
    ject (Southwest), Grey Wolf Restoration Project (Yellowstone
    National Park), Suit vs. United States for failure to enforce
    Endangered Species Act
Periodicals: *Defenders* (magazine)
Reports: Yes

Fish and Wildlife Service
U.S. Department of the Interior
1849 C Street, NW
Washington, DC 20240
Phone: 202-208-5634   Fax: 202-208-5850
John F. Turner, Director
Purpose: The federal agency designated to conserve and protect
    the nation's fish and wildlife and their habitats "for the con-
    tinuing benefit of people." This agency also manages the en-
    dangered species list.
Founded: 1871; became part of the Department of the Interior
    in 1940
FYR: 1990
Revenue: $897,874,000
Expenditures: $832,283,000
Staff: 7,000
Topics: Conservation, endangered species, fish, habitats, wildlife
Approaches: Education, land acquisition, policy, publications,
    research
Scope: National
Reports: Yes

**International Union for the Conservation of Nature and
Natural Resources** (IUCN)
1400 16th Street, NW
Washington, DC 20036
Phone: 202-797-5454   Fax: 202-797-5461
Byron Swift, Executive Director
Purpose: To promote global conservation of biological diversity
    and sustainable development of natural resources.

Founded: 1986
FYR: 1990
Revenue: $367,481
Expenditures: $375,557
Staff: 8
Affiliates: World Conservation Union
Topics: Antarctica, biodiversity, endangered species, marine ecosystems, natural resource management, plant conservation, population, sustainable development, tropical forests, wetlands
Approaches: Education, funding, lobbying, policy
Scope: International

Manomet Bird Observatory
P.O. Box 936
Manomet, MA 02345
Phone: 508-224-6521   Fax: 508-224-9220
Linda E. Leddy, Director
Purpose: To conduct long-term environmental research and education on the ecology and conservation of neotropical migrant land and shorebirds.
Founded: 1969
FYR: 1990
Revenue: $1,976,649
Expenditures: $1,963,604
Staff: 66
Topics: Biodiversity, coastal issues, ecosystems, endangered lands, fisheries, flyways, habitats, marine issues, shorebirds, wetlands
Approaches: Conferences, education, land acquisition, publications, research
Scope: International
Reports: Yes

Missouri Botanical Garden
P.O. Box 299
St. Louis, MO 63166
Phone: 314-577-5100   Fax: 314-577-9597
Peter H. Raven, Director

Purpose: At the forefront of the international biodiversity move-
ment, the Garden works to advance and disseminate knowl-
edge about plants and their aesthetic and environmental
importance.
Founded: 1859
FYR: 1990
Revenue: $12,833,048
Expenditures: $12,476,742
1990 membership: 27,386
Staff: 293
Topics: Biodiversity, horticulture
Approaches: Conferences, education, publications, research
Scope: International
Periodicals: *Annals of the Missouri Botanical Garden* (journal),
Herbarium News (newsletter)
Books: Yes

National Wildlife Federation
1400 16th Street, NW
Washington, DC 20036-2266
Phone: 202-797-6680   Fax: 202-797-6646
Jay D. Hair, President
Purpose: The largest U.S. conservation organization, NWF
works in both traditional conservation areas and the newer
ones such as global climate change. Among NWF's accom-
plishments are its great publications for kids.
Founded: 1936
FYR: 1990
Revenue: $88,669,000
Expenditures: $89,460,000
1990 membership: 5,600,000
Change from 1989: +10%
Staff: 608
Affiliates: 52 state affiliates
Topics: Biodiversity, endangered species, energy, habitats, water
resources
Approaches: Advocacy, education, grassroots organizing, lobby-
ing, publications, research
Scope: National

Periodicals: *Your Big Backyard* (newsletter), *Conservation Exchange* (newsletter), *The Leader* (newspaper), *Ranger Rick* (children's magazine)

RARE Center for Tropical Bird Conservation
1529 Walnut Street
Philadelphia, PA 19102
Phone: 215-568-0420   Fax: 215-568-0516
John E. Earhart, President
Purpose: To ensure the survival of endangered tropical birds and their habitats.
Founded: 1974
FYR: 1990
Revenue: $331,675
Expenditures: $331,675
1990 membership: 1,000
Change from 1989: +10%
Staff: 3
Topics: Biodiversity, birds, endangered lands, habitats, tropical rain forest
Approaches: Direct action, education, land acquisition, publications, research
Scope: International, with a geographic focus on New World tropics
Periodicals: *RARE Center News* (newsletter)

Seed Savers Exchange
Rural Route 3
Box 239
Decorah, IA 52101
Phone: 319-382-5990
Kent Whealey, Director
Purpose: To save old-time food crops from extinction.
Founded: 1975
FYR: 1990
Revenue: Not available
Expenditures: Not available
Staff: 4
Topics: Food crops, genetic diversity, heritage seedstocks

Approaches: Conferences, education, grassroots organizing, publications, research
Scope: International
Special projects: Office at Heritage Farms
Periodicals: *The Yearbook* (journal)
Books: Yes

TRAFFIC USA
1250 24th Street, NW, Suite 500
Washington, DC 20037
Phone: 202-293-4800   Fax: 202-775-8287
Ginette Hemley, Director
Purpose: A program of the World Wildlife Fund set up to disseminate information on international wildlife trade.
Founded: 1979
FYR: 1990
Revenue: Not available
Expenditures: Not available
Staff: 6
Affiliates: World Wildlife Fund and The Conservation Foundation
Topics: Endangered species, illegal wildlife trade
Approaches: Education, publications, research
Scope: International

Trout Unlimited
800 Follin Lane, Suite 250
Vienna, VA 22180-4906
Phone: 703-281-1100   Fax: 703-281-1825
Stephen Lundy, President
Purpose: To conserve, restore, and enhance North America's trout, salmon, and steelhead and their watersheds.
Founded: 1959
FYR: 1990
Revenue: $2,635,968
Expenditures: $3,073,826
1990 membership: 65,000
Change from 1989: +4%
Staff: 20

Chapters: 400
Affiliates: Yes
Topics: Fisheries, recreation, rivers/streams, water quality, watersheds
Approaches: Advocacy, direct action, education, grassroots organizing, land acquisition, publications
Scope: National
Special projects: Embrace-a-Stream
Periodicals: *Trout* (newsletter), *Action Line* (newsletter)
Reports: Yes

Wildlife Conservation International (WCI)
New York Zoological Society
Bronx Zoo
Bronx, NY 10460
Phone: 212-220-5155   Fax: 212-220-7114
John Robinson, Director
Purpose: The field science division of the New York Zoological Society, WCI works to conserve species and biological processes in 125 projects in 40 countries around the world.
Founded: 1897
FYR: 1990
Revenue: [$4,100,000]
Expenditures: $4,095,656
1990 membership: 35,000
Staff: 32
Topics: Coastal issues, conservation, ecosystems, endangered species, ethnobiology, forests, habitats, marine mammals, protected lands, wildlife, zoos/aquariums
Approaches: Conferences, education, publications, research
Scope: International
Periodicals: *Wildlife Conservation* (magazine)
Books: Yes
Reports: Yes

World Wildlife Fund
1250 24th Street, NW
Washington, DC 20037
Phone: 202-293-4800   Fax: 202-293-9211

Kathryn S. Fuller, President

Purpose: Now fully merged with The Conservation Foundation, WWF is the largest U.S. private organization working to protect endangered wildlife and wildlands around the world. Since its founding, WWF has carried out more than 1,600 conservation projects in 107 countries.

Founded: 1961

FYR: 1990

Revenue: $43,857,330

Expenditures: $43,005,077

1990 membership: 1,000,000

Staff: 250

Affiliates: 26 affiliates worldwide

Topics: Biodiversity, conservation, endangered species, habitats, wildlife

Approaches: Advocacy, conferences, education, funding, land acquisition, lobbying, policy, publications, research

Scope: International, with a geographic focus on the tropical forests of Latin America, Africa, and Asia

Periodicals: *Focus* (newsletter), *Traffic USA* (newsletter), *Resolve* (newsletter)

Reports: Yes

Xerces Society

10 Southwest Ash Street

Portland, OR 97204

Phone: 503-222-2788   Fax: 503-222-2763

Jeffrey Glassberg, President

Purpose: Initially formed to preserve butterflies and their habitats, the Society now works on the broader conservation issue of invertebrates and their role in world ecosystems.

Founded: 1971

FYR: 1990

Revenue: $264,007

Expenditures: $249,232

1990 membership: 2,280

Staff: 7

Topics: Biodiversity, ecosystems, endangered species

Approaches: Education, policy, publications, research

Scope: International
Periodicals: *Wings* (magazine), *Atala* (journal)
Reports: Yes

❑ *Foundation Funding*

In 1990, about 15 percent of the dollars contributed for environmental programs by U.S. independent and community foundations went primarily for biodiversity projects.

❑ **ENVIRONMENTAL GRANT-MAKING FOUNDATIONS:** ❑
FUNDING FOR BIODIVERSITY PROJECTS 1990

Rank	Foundation	Number of Grants	Dollars Awarded
1	Hall Family Foundations	1	5,000,000
2	John D. and Catherine T. MacArthur Foundation	20	4,932,750
3	The Pew Charitable Trusts	9	3,599,409
4	Mary Flagler Cary Charitable Trust	3	3,566,466
5	W. Alton Jones Foundation, Inc.	14	1,885,860
6	Lyndhurst Foundation	1	1,250,000
7	The Andrew W. Mellon Foundation	7	1,215,000
8	The Joyce Foundation	7	1,195,000
9	National Fish and Wildlife Foundation	25	1,044,350
10	The Harry and Grace Steele Foundation	2	1,025,000

7

Water

LIFE ON EARTH DEPENDS ON FRESH water, a renewable resource that accounts for less than .01 percent of the Earth's total water. Fresh water includes surface waters (rivers, streams, lakes) and groundwater. Like surface water, groundwater is a renewable resource, but the renewal process takes place over long periods of time.

Water continuously circulates in the hydrologic cycle: evaporating from the oceans, condensing into droplets, precipitating onto the land, and returning again through evaporation to the atmosphere or through runoff to the sea. Some 41,000 cubic kilometers of water are thought to be involved in these processes every year, but only about 9,000 cubic kilometers are available for human use.

Human beings intervene in the water cycle in two ways: (1) by withdrawing large quantities of water from rivers, lakes and aquifers; and (2) by clearing vegetation from land. Deforestation and conversion of natural lands reduce natural seepage into underground aquifers; these activities also increase the rate of surface runoff, which in turn causes soil erosion.

Fresh water is unevenly distributed and consumed around the globe. But even in countries with a plentiful supply, fresh water is becoming increasingly scarce and polluted as population, agriculture, and industry expand. The United States is one of those countries richly endowed with fresh water, but we are now experiencing regional water scarcities. We also have severe water pollution nationwide.

WATER SCARCITY

Worldwide, agriculture represents the most serious threat to water supplies. Agriculture accounts for 73 percent of consumptive water use throughout the world (60 percent in the United States) and irrigated land is increasing at 8 percent per year.

The United States may use more water per capita than any other nation. A 1980 survey documented U.S. withdrawals at 7,200 liters per person as compared to 4,800 liters per person in Canada, 3,600 in the USSR, and 1,400 in the United Kingdom.

It is estimated that one-fifth of the water pumped out of the ground each year in the United States is essentially nonrenewable. In parts of the Great Plains and the Southwest, groundwater is being drawn out more rapidly than it can be replenished. The Ogallala aquifer, which supplies water to one-fifth of all U.S. irrigated cropland, is already half depleted. The overdraft of this aquifer each year nearly equals the annual water flow of the Colorado River.

Damage to a drawn-down aquifer can be irreversible. Groundwater overdraft can cause "subsidence," or irreversible settling of the land resulting in aquifer collapse as the water is removed. A collapsed aquifer can never be replenished.

As scarcity increases, the problem becomes not only where to go for more water but how to better manage existing resources. Solutions include a different allocation of uses and efforts at conservation.

One method of coping with scarcity is *reallocation* of water resources from one region to another, either by government regulation or by water marketing. In the arid southwestern United States, scarce water is increasingly reallocated from agriculture to cities and industry.

Conservation efforts may be a better way of dealing with water scarcity, since they are directed at the root problem—overuse. Conservation strategies include:

- *Pricing.* A shift in pricing can encourage big users to cut water consumption. Historically, government subsidies have underpriced water relative to its costs. Until recently, farmers in the western United States paid only 16 percent of what it cost the government to provide water for irrigation. New cost-sharing requirements are beginning to rectify this situation, at least in the case of new projects, where beneficiaries now have to pay 35 percent of construction costs.

- *Efficiency measures.* Agricultural irrigation offers the greatest potential for an increase in efficiency. Since 1950, the area of irrigated land worldwide has tripled. One-third of the world's food is now grown on irrigated lands, which account for 18 percent of all cropland. A number of techniques can make irrigation more efficient: one of the best is microirrigation, where small amounts of water are applied directly to the roots of crops.

- *Water reuse.* Japan, China and Israel all have successful models for cleansing and recirculating wastewater. In the United States, we habitually squander vast quantities of water on our lawns, ourselves, our dishes, and waste disposal. In the arid West, treated wastewater is frequently used to irrigate crops, parks, and golf courses. But more complete water reclamation is possible. Ocean Arks of Falmouth, Massachusetts, has developed a prototype for recycling sewage water within a dwelling, community, or urban area. This system is now being used to treat municipal sewage in Harwich, Massachusetts, and Providence, Rhode Island.

WATER QUALITY

Water pollution can be characterized by its origin. *Point-source pollution* emanates from a discrete and identifiable source such as a municipal sewage system or an industrial plant. *Nonpoint-source pollution* includes diffuse runoff from agricultural fields or urban streets. Considerable progress has been made over the past 25 years in controlling point-source pollution. Nonpoint-source pollution is recognized today as a much more serious threat to water quality, in part because it is so difficult to control.

Ground and surface waters in the United States are polluted from both land and atmospheric sources. Land sources can be either point or nonpoint. By definition, atmospheric entry (such as acid deposition created by vehicular and industrial exhausts or heavy metals dispersed in the air from waste incineration) is nonpoint.

Pollutants include natural contaminants (human, animal, and vegetative waste) and industrial contaminants. Among the most important human activities contributing to water pollution are:

- *Agriculture,* by far the biggest source of water pollution.

- *Deforestation,* which increases soil runoff and erosion.

- *Industrial wastes* such as heavy metals and PCBs, which accumulate in the bottom mud of lakes and rivers.

- *Mining wastes,* which contain heavy metals that leach into streams near abandoned mines in the western mountains, especially the Rockies, Cascades, and Sierra Nevadas. Acid deposition compounds the problem.

- *Atmospheric deposition* of substances such as fly ash from incinerators, sprayed pesticides, nitrous oxides, and sulfur dioxide from industrial and vehicular emissions. These fall into fresh waters, creating acidity.

- *Urban runoff,* which includes everything from sulfuric and nitric acids, copper, zinc, vanadium, hydrocarbons, phosphates, asbestos, particulates, lead, chlorides, chromates, cyanides, and organic chemicals to untreated garbage. The scope of the urban runoff problem is not well understood.

Pollution can affect both surface and ground water. Severely polluted surface waters are known as impacted waters. In the United States, 9 percent of the total 1.8 million miles of rivers are impacted; 21 percent of a total 39.4 million acres of lakes are impacted. Agricultural runoff is the major factor in 64 percent of the polluted rivers and 7 percent of the polluted lakes.

A more serious problem is the pollution of groundwater, which is a significant source of drinking water in the United States. Pollutants enter groundwater as seepage from waste dumps, leakage from sewers and fuel tanks, and runoff from agricultural land or paved surfaces in urban areas. Cut off from the atmosphere's oxygen, groundwater has a low capacity for self-purification.

Present concern about groundwater centers on nitrates and pesticides, both of which potentially threaten human health. At least 5 to 10 percent of U.S. groundwater has nitrate concentrations that exceed the Environmental Protection Agency (EPA) standard of 45 mg/liter. In 1980, pesticide contamination was found in groundwater stores in 40 states. The EPA is currently completing a national survey of groundwater contamination by 100 pesticide residues. Final results should be available by early 1992.

In April 1991, based on preliminary results, the EPA proposed scientific criteria for restricting certain categories of pesticides. Under this plan, the EPA would screen pesticides and consider classifying them as restricted-use if any of the ingredients are "persistent and mobile" and therefore likely to leach into the soil and groundwater, or if they have already been detected in groundwater in three or more U.S. counties. In the past, the federal government has not been considered a leader in pesticide control, and has actually inhibited efforts by some states to restrict pesticide use within their borders. Recently the Supreme Court awarded the states the right to regulate pesticides more stringently than the federal government.

Water quality in the United States is a particularly difficult issue, because there is no single agency in charge. The EPA, the U.S. Geological Survey, the National Oceanic and Atmospheric Administration, the Fish and Wildlife Service, and the National Aeronautics and Space Administration all share responsibility for water quality.

OTHER WATER ISSUES

There are other water issues besides water quantity and water quality. One is rivers. The United States has 3.5 million miles of rivers. Once all were free-flowing. Now 600,000 miles (about 17 percent) are stilled by concrete dams. Additional thousands of miles have been straightened or dredged in our zeal to control natural systems. Each of these interferences has contributed to a loss of trout and salmon fisheries, white-water runs, and habitats of endangered aquatic and stream-bank species. Aquatic species in North America are believed to be declining faster than land-based species. According to The Nature Conservancy, one-third of the continent's fish, two-thirds of its crayfish, and nearly three-quarters of its mussels are in jeopardy.

Permanent protection for rivers can be attained through the Wild and Scenic Rivers Act, which was passed in 1968. As of January 1992, wild and scenic status had been granted to 125 river segments totaling 9,452 miles in 32 states.

River protection includes not only in-stream issues, but also riparian ecosystems—the wetlands, streamside forests, and up-lands adjacent to rivers and streams. These lands extend to the borders of the floodplain and are usually dependent on periodic flooding. They are among the richest ecosystems known.

The United States has 121 million acres of riparian lands. Today only about 23 million acres are in their natural or semi-natural state. Seventy percent of the original floodplain forests have been converted to urban or cultivated agricultural uses. The rest have been cleared of natural vegetation, paved, or turned into housing developments and shopping malls.

RESOURCES

✿ Books and Reports

Conserving Water: The Untapped Alternative. Worldwatch Paper 67. Sandra Postel. Washington, DC: Worldwatch Institute. 1985, 66 pp.

Down by the River: The Impact of Federal Water Projects and Policies on Biological Diversity. Constance Elizabeth Hunt in cooperation with the National Wildlife Federation. Washington, DC: Island Press. 1988, 266 pp.

Groundwater: A Community Action Guide. Washington, DC: Concern, Inc. 1989, 22 pp.

Local Groundwater Protection. Martin Jaffe and Frank Dinovo. Chicago: American Planning Association. 1987, 262 pp.

National Water Summary 1987: Hydrologic Events and Ground-Water Quality. U.S. Geological Survey Water-Supply Paper 2325. Washington, DC: U.S. Government Printing Office. 1989, 551 pp.

Pesticides and Groundwater Quality: Issues and Problems in Four States. Washington, DC: National Academy Press. 1986, 124 pp.

The Poisoned Well. Sierra Club Legal Defense Fund, Eric P. Jorgensen, editor. Washington, DC: Island Press. 1989, 415 pp.

Redefining National Water Policy: New Roles and Directions. Stephen M. Born, editor. Bethesda, MD: American Water Resources Association. 1989, 93 pp.

Rivers at Risk: The Concerned Citizen's Guide to Hydropower. John D. Echeverria, Pope Barrow, and Richard Roos-Collins. American Rivers. Washington, DC: Island Press. 1989, 216 pp.

Saving Water from the Ground Up: A Pilot Study of Irrigation Scheduling on Four California Fields. Gail Richardson. New York: INFORM. 1985, 64 pp.

Skimming the Water: Rent-seeking and the Performance of Public Irrigation Systems. Washington, DC: World Resources Institute. 1986, 46 pp.

The Snake River: Window to the West. Tim Palmer. Washington, DC: Island Press, 1991, 300 pp.

Turning the Tide: Saving the Chesapeake Bay. Tom Horton and William M. Eichbaum. The Chesapeake Bay Foundation. Washington, DC: Island Press. 1991, 327 pp.

We All Live Downstream: A Guide to Waste Treatment that Stops Water Pollution. Pat Costner. Eureka Springs, AR: Waterworks Publishing Company. 1986, 91 pp.

✪ Periodicals

American Rivers
American Rivers
801 Pennsylvania Avenue, SE, Suite 303
Washington, DC 20003
Phone: 202-547-6900   Fax: 202-543-6142
Randy Showstack, Editor
Type: Magazine
Frequency: Quarterly
Length: 20 pp.
Subscription fee: Free with membership
Topics: Policy, protection of rivers/streams, recreation, riparian development, wilderness
Coverage: Book reviews, business/industry, organization activities
Audience: Citizens, environmental organizations
Scope: National
Comment: Covers achievements in river protection by American Rivers, one of the principal river-saving organizations in the United States. Includes reports on federal and state legislation and special features such as vignettes of choice river trips.

Arroyo
University of Arizona
Water Resources Research Center
Tucson, AZ 85721
Phone: 602-621-7607   Fax: 602-792-8518
Joe Gelt, Editor
Type: Newsletter
Frequency: Quarterly
Length: 8 pp.
Subscription fee: Free
Topics: Drylands, water policy and use
Coverage: Organization activities, research
Audience: Citizens
Scope: State
Comment: Reports scientific research on Arizona water issues in a way that is accessible to the nonscientist.

Clean Water Action News
Clean Water Action, Inc.
1320 18th Street, NW, 3rd Floor
Washington, DC 20036
Phone: 202-457-1286   Fax: 202-457-0287
David Zwick, Executive Editor
Type: Newsletter
Frequency: Quarterly
Length: 16 pp.
Subscription fee: $24
Topics: Pesticides, toxics, water quality, waste
Coverage: Activism, environmental community, organization activities
Audience: Citizens, environmental organizations
Scope: National
Advertising: Yes
Comment: State and national news about a range of environmental issues and events, often dealing with water. Typical articles: "Getting Tough on Environmental Crime," "Saving Water and Dollars: An Earth Day Message."

Focus on International Joint Commission Activities
International Joint Commission
Great Lakes Regional Office
P.O. Box 32869
Detroit, MI 48232-2869
Phone: 313-226-2170   Fax: 519-256-7791
Sally Cole-Misch, Editor
Type: Newsletter
Frequency: 3 issues per year
Length: 30 pp.
Subscription fee: Free
Topics: Lakes, pollution, water quality
Coverage: Organization activities
Audience: Citizens, government
Scope: Regional (Great Lakes)
Comment: About activities of the International Joint Commission that monitors the Great Lakes ecosystem in the United States and Canada.

The Great Lakes United
Great Lakes United
c/o David Miller
24 Agassiz Circle
Buffalo, NY 14214
Phone: 716-886-0142
Bruce Kershner, Editor
Type: Newsletter
Frequency: Quarterly
Length: 8 pp.
Subscription fee: Free with membership
Topics: Lakes, toxics, water quality, wetlands
Coverage: Business/industry, environmental community
Audience: Citizens
Scope: Regional (Great Lakes)
Comment: An important source of information on Great Lakes problems and solutions.

Headwaters
Friends of the River Foundation
Fort Mason Center

Building C
San Francisco, CA 94123
Phone: 415-771-0400   Fax: 415-771-0301
Ted Cuzzillo, Editor
Type: Newsletter
Frequency: Bimonthly
Length: 24 pp.
Subscription fee: Free with membership
Topics: Recreation, rivers/streams, water quality
Coverage: Policy
Audience: Citizens
Scope: Regional (western United States)
Advertising: Yes
Comment: Convincing arguments for maintaining rivers in their
    wild and beautiful state.

❖ Organizations

The American Groundwater Trust
6375 Riverside Drive
Dublin, OH 43017
Phone: 614-761-2215   Fax: 614-761-3446
Kevin B. McCray, Executive Director
Purpose: To promote public awareness about problems of
    groundwater overuse and contamination.
Founded: 1975
FYR: 1990
Revenue: $212,808
Expenditures: $110,454
Staff: 2
Affiliates: Nebraska Groundwater Foundation, National Water
    Well Association (parent organization)
Topics: Groundwater protection, water resources
Approaches: Conferences, education, publications, research
Scope: National
Special projects: National Groundwater Information Center,
    Scholarship Program
Periodicals: *Points* (newsletter)
Reports: Yes

American Rivers

801 Pennsylvania Avenue, SE, Suite 303
Washington, DC 20003
Phone: 202-547-6900   Fax: 202-543-6142
Kevin J. Coyle, President
Purpose: To preserve the nation's outstanding rivers and their landscapes in their natural state and protect them from the many forces that conspire to degrade them.
Founded: 1973
FYR: 1990
Revenue: [$1,556,000]
Expenditures: [$1,553,000]
1990 membership: 15,000
Change from 1989: +15%
Staff: 18
Topics: Biodiversity; in-stream issues; river policy, planning, and protection; wilderness
Approaches: Advocacy, conferences, direct action, education, grassroots organizing, legislation, litigation, policy, publications
Scope: National
Special projects: Wild and Scenic Rivers Designation, Hydropower Policy, Rivers of High Biodiversity
Periodicals: *American Rivers* (magazine)
Reports: Yes

American Water Resources Association

5410 Grosvenor Lane, Suite 220
Bethesda, MD 20814
Phone: 301-493-8600   Fax: 301-493-5844
Warren Viessman, Jr., President
Purpose: To advance interdisciplinary water resources research, planning, management, development and education.
Founded: 1964
FYR: 1990
Revenue: $626,621
Expenditures: $626,621
1990 membership: 3,400
Staff: 5

Topics: Water resources
Approaches: Conferences, education, publications
Scope: National
Periodicals: *The Water Resources Bulletin* (journal), *The High Data: News and Views* (newsletter)
Reports: Yes

The Center for the Great Lakes

435 N. Michigan Avenue, Suite 1408
Chicago, IL 60611
Phone: 312-263-0785   Fax: 312-201-0683
Daniel K. Ray, Director
Purpose: To foster regional cooperation among political, business, and environmental leaders on both sides of the U.S./Canadian border on critical natural resource and economic issues, and to promote public awareness and understanding about them.
Founded: 1983
FYR: 1990
Revenue: $615,183
Expenditures: $605,430
Staff: 10
Topics: Development, ecosystems, hazardous substances, lakes, water quality, watersheds
Approaches: Conferences, education, policy, publications, research
Scope: Regional (Great Lakes)
Special projects: Pollution Prevention Program, Environment and Economy Coordination, Great Lakes Heritage Areas
Periodicals: *Great Lakes Reporter* (newsletter)
Books: Yes
Reports: Yes

Chesapeake Bay Trust

60 West Street, Suite 200-A
Annapolis, MD 21401
Phone: 301-974-2941   Fax: 301-269-0387
Thomas L. Burden, Executive Director
Purpose: To engage the public in efforts to restore and protect

Chesapeake Bay by awarding grants to civic and community organizations, environmental groups, schools, and public agencies.
Founded: 1985
FYR: 1990
Revenue: $782,164
Expenditures: $481,423
Staff: 4
Topics: Coastal issues, endangered species, marine issues, watershed preservation and restoration
Approaches: Funding
Scope: Regional (Chesapeake Bay watershed)

Clean Water Action, Inc.
317 Pennsylvania Avenue, SE
Washington, DC 20003-0884
Phone: 202-547-1196   Fax: 202-457-0287
David Zwick, Executive Director
Purpose: To promote natural resource protection through control of toxic chemicals, safe solid waste management practices, and protection of wetlands, surface waters, coastal areas, and groundwater.
Founded: 1971
FYR: 1990
Revenue: $11,666,294
Expenditures: $11,633,284
1990 membership: 600,000
Staff: 1,000
Chapters: 26
Topics: Drinking water, groundwater, hazardous substances and waste, lakes, recycling, rivers/streams
Approaches: Direct action, education, grassroots organizing, lobbying, publications, research
Scope: National
Special projects: The War on Waste Campaign
Periodicals: *Clean Water Action News* (newsletter), *Sustain Our Water* (bulletin), *News You Can Use* (newsletter)
Reports: Yes
Books: Yes

Freshwater Foundation
725 Country Road Six
Wayzata, MN 55391
Phone: 612-449-0092   Fax: 612-449-0592
Martin Jessen, President
Purpose: Research and education to keep freshwater resources usable for human consumption, industry, and recreation.
Founded: 1968
FYR: 1990
Revenue: $987,576
Expenditures: $955,035
1990 membership: 1,600
Staff: 11
Topics: Groundwater, preservation of lakes and water resources, surface water
Approaches: Conferences, education, policy, publications, research
Scope: National
Special projects: Lake and Wetlands Project
Periodicals: *Facets of Freshwater* (newsletter), *U.S. Water News* (journal), *Health & Environment Digest* (newsletter)
Reports: Yes

Friends of the River
Fort Mason Center, Building C
San Francisco, CA 94123
Phone: 415-771-0400
David M. Bolling, Executive Director
Purpose: To protect and restore rivers throughout the West and to shape new water policies that balance development with preservation. Its primary audience is the outdoors enthusiast.
Founded: 1974
FYR: 1990
Revenue: [$750,000]
Expenditures: [$750,000]
1990 membership: 10,000
Staff: 5
Affiliates: Friends of the River Foundation
Topics: Fisheries, in-stream issues and protection, recreation, rivers/streams

Approaches: Grassroots organizing, lobbying, policy, publications
Scope: Regional (western United States)
Periodicals: *Headwaters* (newsletter), *Cross-Current* (newsletter)

Great Lakes United
Buffalo State College
Cassety Hall
1300 Elmwood Avenue
Buffalo, NY 14222
Phone: 716-886-0142   Fax: 716-886-0303
Frederick L. Brown, President
Purpose: This umbrella organization for a coalition of U.S. and Canadian environmental, industrial and governmental groups works to preserve the Great Lakes and St. Lawrence River ecosystem.
Founded: 1982
FYR: 1989
Revenue: $176,772
Expenditures: $216,549
1990 membership: 1,000
Staff: 6
Topics: Ecosystem planning and regulation, preservation of lakes
Approaches: Advocacy, conferences, education, grassroots organizing, legislation, policy, publications, research, technical assistance
Scope: Regional (Great Lakes)
Special projects: The Zero Discharge Pollution Prevention Campaign
Periodicals: *The Great Lakes United* (newsletter)
Reports: Yes

North American Lake Management Society
One Progress Boulevard, Box 27
Alachua, FL 32615-9536
Phone: 904-462-2554   Fax: 904-462-2568
Richard S. McVoy, President
Purpose: To promote the understanding, protection, restoration and management of lakes, ponds, and reservoirs.

Founded: 1980
FYR: 1990
Revenue: $525,421
Expenditures: $512,553
1990 membership: 2,300
Staff: 3
Chapters: 11
Topics: Lake eutrophication, preservation, and sedimentation, water quality
Approaches: Conferences, education, policy, publications, research
Scope: National
Periodicals: *Lake and Reservoir Management* (journal), *Lake Line* (newsletter)
Reports: Yes

Ocean Arks International

One Locust Street
Falmouth, MA 02540
Phone: 508-540-6801   Fax: 508-540-6811
John Todd, Director
Purpose: With the goal of restoring the Earth's water to its original condition, Ocean Arks uses natural biologic filtration systems to purify sewage on a local or municipal level.
Founded: 1981
FYR: 1990
Revenue: $590,000
Expenditures: $470,000
1990 membership: 3,000
Staff: 10
Topics: Wastewater treatment, water conservation and purification
Approaches: Conferences, education, funding, publications, research
Scope: International
Special projects: Use of the solar aquatic waste treatment method in several northeastern urban areas
Periodicals: *Annals of Earth* (newsletter)

River Network
P.O. Box 8787
Portland, OR 97207
Phone: 503-241-3506
Phillip Wallin, Director
Purpose: To protect outstanding American river systems. River Network works through citizen training and river/land acquisition, taking an ecosystem view of river preservation.
Founded: 1987
FYR: 1990
Revenue: $163,152
Expenditures: $161,692
Staff: 3
Topics: Biodiversity, recreation, rivers/streams, watersheds, wetlands, wildlife
Approaches: Advocacy, grassroots organizing, land acquisition
Scope: National
Special projects: River clearinghouse
Periodicals: *River Network Bulletin* (newsletter)

❏ Foundation Funding

In 1990, about 7 percent of the dollars awarded by U.S. independent and community foundations for environmental programs went for water projects.

❏ **ENVIRONMENTAL GRANT-MAKING FOUNDATIONS: FUNDING FOR WATER PROJECTS 1990** ❏

Rank	Foundation	Number of Grants	Dollars Awarded
1	W. K. Kellogg Foundation	13	3,222,784
2	The Ford Foundation	23	1,916,000
3	The Joyce Foundation	16	1,303,894
4	Jessie Smith Noyes Foundation, Inc.	29	1,280,000
5	The William Penn Foundation	3	1,125,000
6	Northwest Area Foundation	5	846,430
7	Charles Stewart Mott Foundation	15	794,581
8	Lyndhurst Foundation	1	700,000
9	The Blandin Foundation	2	489,500
10	The Pew Charitable Trusts	5	462,000

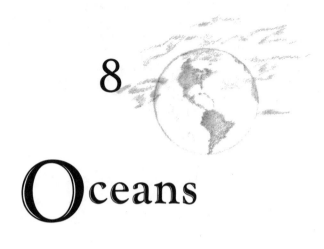

8

Oceans

OUR PLANET MIGHT BETTER BE named Oceana than Earth, since oceans cover 70 percent of its surface. Oceans carry out a wide range of biological functions essential for life. They regulate the climate by helping distribute solar heat and absorbing carbon dioxide. They also provide habitat for more than 250,000 species of marine plants and animals and one-quarter of the animal protein humans use for food.

The coasts are the most productive—and vulnerable—of the ocean regions. Warm, nutrient-rich shallows over the continental shelves nurture the great fisheries: Over 99 percent of the world's marine catch is taken within 320 kilometers of a coast. These shallows, where fresh water mixes with salt and up-welling occurs, account for less than 10 percent of the oceans' total area, yet are home for 90 percent of their plant and animal life.

Coastal zone estuaries, a subregion of the shallows, produce more plant biomass per square foot than any other ecosystem on Earth. Estuaries and coastal wetlands dilute and filter out large amounts of waterborne pollutants. They act as protective barriers for coastal lands. They are also spawning grounds and feeding or nursery areas for most marine fish.

Human populations too tend to congregate along coasts, and coastal zones bear the brunt of human activities. In the United States, about 60 percent of the population lives along a coast of the Atlantic, the Pacific, or the Great Lakes. By 1995, 75 to 80 percent of Americans will live on or near a coast. Worldwide, more than half the human population lives on coastal lands or river deltas, or along estuaries.

This concentration of humans and their activities along coasts is wreaking havoc on coastal and marine ecosystems. Building (or even walking) on fragile dunes near the shore can destroy these natural barriers, exposing delicate ecosystems to the open ocean. Coastal development also typically degrades wetlands such as salt marshes and mangroves.

Mangrove ecosystems are linked with coral reefs, which scientists consider the marine equivalent of tropical rain forests in the richness of species they shelter. Worldwide, as mangroves succumb to development, coral reefs are threatened by a host of factors. These include: mangrove loss; silt from eroded soils and chemical pollution; anchor damage; plunder by trophy hunters and dynamite by fishermen; and climate change.

Human activities other than development impinge on marine environments. The results of such activities include:

- Species exploitation;
- Pollution; and
- Climate change.

SPECIES EXPLOITATION

Marine mammals, fish, and plant life are all increasingly subject to overharvest as more and more people cast their nets into the same seas. Although the plight of marine mammals has received the most publicity, the decline of world fisheries may be a more fundamental problem.

Seventy-one percent of the world's fish is supplied by commercial fisheries; 87 percent of that comes from the oceans. Five countries—Chile, China, Japan, the former USSR, and the United States—account for about half the total catch.

Over the last four decades, a dangerous trend can be observed:

- Between 1950 and 1970, the annual commercial fish catch increased from 23 million to 68 million metric tons.
- Between 1980 and 1990, the annual global catch increased by 30 percent. By 1986, the catch was 84 million metric tons.
- By 1990, 255 of the 280 fish stocks tracked by the United Nations Food and Agriculture Organization (FAO) were considered "moderately" or "heavily" exploited.
- The annual catch is now close to 100 million metric tons, which most experts believe is the maximum sustainable yield.

Overfishing can lead to the kind of population crashes that have been seen off the east coast of the United States. In 1976, the United States extended its territorial waters from three to 200 miles offshore, in part to curb overfishing by foreign fleets. At that time there were approximately 590 U.S. vessels bringing in 250 million pounds of groundfish each year. By the early 1980s, the number of vessels had mushroomed to 1,000 and the annual catch had increased to 410 million pounds. At that time catch quotas and trip limits were lifted, resulting in a free-for-all atmosphere and serious depletion of fish stocks. Overfishing has now reduced the eastern seaboard catch to less than 200 million pounds per year. The fishing economy is suffering greatly with boat owners now forced to fish more hours per day or to sell out when they can't make ends meet.

A number of modern fishing techniques contribute to overexploitation, but drift nets are of particular concern. Mesh curtains of nearly invisible plastic line, drift nets dangle to depths of 30 feet, snaring everything that swims by. As much as 70 percent of the total catch in a drift net is "bycatch" or species that are discarded. This includes an estimated 120,000 dolphins and 800,000 seabirds each year.

Nonexistent in the late 1970s, the population of drift net boats exploded after huge stocks of neon flying squid were discovered. By 1983, some 700 vessels deploying a million miles of net a year were fishing for squid in the colder waters of the North Pacific. As of 1991, more than 1,000 Japanese, Taiwanese, and South Korean boats were dragging the high seas with nets 25 miles long.

A UN resolution has called for a moratorium on drift netting in 1992 (except when "conservation and management measures are adopted"). Under threat of U.S. economic sanctions, Japan has declared its intention to discontinue the practice.

POLLUTION

Oceans are the ultimate sink for much of the waste humans produce. Rivers load the oceans with chemicals, nutrients, and particulate matter from agricultural and urban runoff, atmospheric fallout, garbage, and sewage. Ships dump sludge and trash. Tankers and offshore drilling platforms release oil in accidental spills or in intentional discharges when tankers empty or clean their bilges. The range of sources of pollution is staggering.

Nonpoint-source pollution (from agriculture and industry) accounts for at least one-third of U.S. coastal pollution:

- *Agricultural waste.* Thirteen billion tons of silt flow from river mouths into coastal zones each year as runoff from agricultural lands. Deforestation and poor agricultural practices accelerate soil erosion; the resulting sedimentation in coastal regions can bury marine ecosystems. Agricultural chemicals are carried along with the sediment.

- *Industrial waste.* Nine major U.S. cities, most of our large ports, about 40 percent of manufacturing plants, and two-thirds of nuclear and coal-fired power plants are situated on coasts. These urban and industrial sources release synthetic organic compounds such as PCBs and pesticides and heavy metals such as mercury into the soils and surface waters that empty into coastal waters.

- *Atmospheric deposition.* Toxic gases and particles discharged into the atmosphere may eventually settle out over the oceans. Sources of atmospheric pollution include one-time events such as the Kuwaiti oil-well conflagration and ongoing processes such as acid deposition. The idea that acid rain could alter the chemistry of our vast oceans may seem farfetched, but is supported by a 1989 study by the Environmental Defense Fund, which found significant acidification of Chesapeake Bay, attributed primarily to acid rain.

Point-source pollution includes solid waste, sewage, and oil.

- *Solid waste.* The United States is thought to contribute about one-third of all the waste dumped into the oceans, although there is no single estimate of total tonnage. Merchant and fishing boats, passenger vessels, and pleasure craft dump an estimated 14 billion pounds of litter into the oceans each year. Much of this is plastic: Merchant ships toss an estimated 450,000 plastic containers in the oceans every day. Plastics may take 50 years or more to break down. Meanwhile, marine mammals and fish routinely swallow or become entangled in them. An estimated 2 million seabirds and more than 100,000 marine mammals are trapped and killed by plastics each year.

   Since December 31, 1988, Annex V of the International Convention for the Prevention of Pollution from Ships (MARPOL) has prohibited ships from dumping plastics at sea. Thus far, the amount of trash on U.S. beaches appears undiminished. The Center for Marine Conservation has sponsored an annual beach cleanup since 1988. In autumn 1990, volunteers in twenty-three U.S. coastal states, the District of Columbia, three inland states, three U.S. territories, and four foreign countries removed 4,375,567 items of trash weighing several hundred tons from over 4,000 miles of beach. Plastic was the greatest culprit, accounting for nearly two-thirds of the items, just as it had been in previous years.

In some areas ocean dumping of incinerator ash is a major problem. Several European countries routinely burn solid and toxic wastes and deposit the residual ash into the North Sea.

- *Sewage.* Every day, barges dump thousands of tons of municipal sludge from New York and New Jersey in the New York Bight, 110 miles off the New Jersey coast. Although this practice became illegal on January 1, 1992, it can continue as long as the dumpers are willing to pay the fines.

  Sewage loads coastal regions with excess nutrients. These nutrients overstimulate marine algae, causing algal blooms and the red and green tides that are becoming a seasonal phenomenon in many parts of the world. In a process called "eutrophication," overpopulated algae deplete oxygen supplies, suffocating fish, plants, and other marine life. Eutrophication has recently been documented in many coastal regions, including the North and South Atlantic, the Mediterranean, the Adriatic, and the western Pacific.

  Sewage also teams with human pathogens—bacteria and viruses. By the late 1980s, 27 percent of U.S. coastal waters around the lower 48 states were closed to shellfish harvesters because of pollution. By 1991, sewage had forced permanent closure of about half the U.S. shellfish beds.

- *Oil.* One-tenth of one percent of the world's total annual oil production (an estimated 5 million tons) makes its way into ocean waters each year. Most of it comes from runoff and minor leaks rather than major catastrophes like the *Exxon Valdez* tanker accident. Oil eventually biodegrades but the process may take months or years depending on factors ranging from the volatility of the type of oil (e.g., fuel or crude) to the temperature and turbulence of the waters. In relatively sheltered estuaries, the breakdown may take decades. Sediments in Massachusetts' Buzzards Bay, for instance, have been found to contain large residues from an oil spill over 20 years ago.

Oceans can dilute, disperse, and degrade large amounts of sewage, sludge, and some types of industrial waste, depending on the concentrations they face. But even the oceans have a limited capacity, and we are now threatening those limits.

In 1990, an international scientific study group, the Group of Experts on the Scientific Aspects of Marine Pollution (GESAMP), wrote a major report on the health of the oceans. Not surprisingly, it concluded that although the open ocean is still fairly healthy, many coastal areas are severely polluted. It determined that a major international effort of unprecedented scope would be required to stem the growing volume and number of human threats to marine life.

CLIMATE CHANGE

Global warming and ozone depletion threaten both marine and land-based life. Global warming, if it occurs, may cause polar ice to melt, raising sea levels and drowning coastal ecosystems. Human populations will also be affected. A rise in sea level would threaten deltas and much of the entire 19,000-mile U.S. coastline. But even with houses strung up and down our shores, damage in the United States would pale in comparison to what is forecast for other nations. Bangladesh offers what is perhaps the worst-case scenario, but it is one well worth citing.

Eighty percent of Bangladesh lies in the Bengal Delta. Efforts to dam and channel its three great river systems, combined with an increased reliance upon groundwater, are already reducing sedimentation and causing subsidence in the delta. By 2050, sea level along the Bengal Coast could rise by as much as 82 inches, to claim 18 percent of the country's habitable land. Under such a scenario, more than 17 million people would lose their homes. In turn, they would create a second flood—of environmental refugees. By 2100, the number of homeless Bangladeshis could climb to 38 million—about four times the 1990 population of New York City.

Stratospheric ozone depletion is also likely to adversely affect marine life. In Antarctica, where the most severe seasonal ozone "hole" occurs, scientists predict that increased exposure to ultraviolet radiation will reduce essential populations of marine organisms such as algae and phytoplankton. A decline in food supply will eventually adversely affect other populations in the marine food web such as seals, penguins, and whales.

Coral reefs, the species-rich gardens of tropical seas, may already be affected by climate change. Coral bleaching, a new and mysterious phenomenon now found in many parts of the world, has been linked with temperature change and increasing ultraviolet radiation.

THE COMMONS

Together with the atmosphere, the oceans are part of the world's commons—resource areas beyond the jurisdiction of any single government. Exploited by all yet protected by few, the oceans are plundered and polluted by a world of nations still largely unable to work together for the common good.

A number of international agreements that address marine resource issues are already in place. Like domestic regulations, these agreements generally take one of three approaches: (1) territorial imperatives, (2) season or species restrictions, or (3) equipment limitations. It is not altogether clear how well any of them work.

One of the most important international agreements on the books is the UN Convention of the Law of the Sea. Written in 1982, the convention awards coastal countries legal rights over all marine fishery and ocean mineral resources in an exclusive economic zone extending 200 nautical miles from the shore, while protecting navigation rights through the zones. This treaty effectively places 40 percent of the world's oceans under the control of individual countries and theoretically could begin to resolve the problem of fishery overexploitation. The deep seabed resources, including minerals, are designated as "the common heritage of mankind."

As of 1990, the convention had been signed by 159 nations, but ratified by just 40. The United States, the United Kingdom, and Germany have thus far declined to participate. The United States supports the concept of exclusive economic zones. Its objections center around the necessity for the developed nations to share the seabed mineral wealth with the developing nations, which otherwise would not have the means to exploit it. Some policy analysts believe the administration's reluctance stems from a fundamental fear that the treaty would set a precedent for world government and the redistribution of wealth.

RESOURCES

☞ Books and Reports

The Beaches Are Moving. Wallace Kaufman and Orrin H. Pilkey, Jr. Durham, NC: Duke University Press. 1983, 143 pp.

A Citizen's Guide to Plastics in the Ocean. Washington, DC: Center for Marine Conservation.1988, 143 pp.

The Law of the Sea: Protection and Preservation of the Marine Environment. United Nations Office for Ocean Affairs and the Law of the Sea. New York: United Nations. 1990, 93 pp.

Life and Death of the Salt Marsh. John and Mildred Teal. Boston: Little, Brown and Company. 1969, 274 pp.

The Living Ocean: Understanding and Protecting Marine Biodiversity. Boyce L. Thorne-Miller and John G. Catena. Washington, DC: Island Press. 1991, 180 pp.

Oil in the Sea: Inputs, Fates, and Effects. Washington, DC: National Academy Press. 1985, 601 pp.

The Sea Around Us. Rachel Carson. New York: Oxford University Press. 1989 edition, 243 pp.

The State of the Marine Environment. Group of Experts on the Scientific Aspects of Marine Pollution (GESAMP). Nairobi: UNEP. 1990, 111 pp.

Under the Sea Wind. Rachel Carson. New York: Truman Tally Books-Dutton. 1991 edition, 304 pp.

The Wasted Ocean. David K. Bulloch. New York: Lyons & Burford. 1989, 150 pp.

Wastes in Marine Environments. Office of Technology Task Force. Cambridge, MA: Hemisphere Publishing Corporation. 1988, 312 pp.

❂ Periodicals

Coastal Connections
Center for Marine Conservation
1725 DeSales Street, NW, Suite 500
Washington, DC 20036
Phone: 202-429-5609   Fax: 202-872-0619
Patty Debenham, Editor
Type: Newsletter
Frequency: 3 issues per year
Length: 7 pp.
Subscription fee: Free
Topics: Coastal issues, litter, marine issues, pollution
Coverage: Activism, organization activities, policy
Audience: Citizens, educators
Scope: National

Greenpeace Magazine
Greenpeace USA
1436 U Street, NW
Washington, DC 20009
Phone: 202-462-1177   Fax: 202-462-4507
Andre Carothers, Editor
Type: Magazine
Frequency: Bimonthly

Length: 28 pp.
Subscription fee: $15
Topics: Climate change, coastal issues, endangered species, fisheries, forests, illegal wildlife trade, marine issues, marine mammals, nuclear issues, solid waste incineration
Coverage: Activism, environmental community, policy, research
Audience: Citizens, environmental organizations
Scope: Global
Comment: Greenpeace now covers all environmental issues, but gives special attention to marine topics (and toxics).

Marine Conservation News
Center for Marine Conservation
1725 DeSales Street, NW, Suite 500
Washington, DC 20036
Phone: 202-429-5609   Fax: 202-872-0619
Rose Bierce, Editor
Type: Newsletter
Frequency: Quarterly
Length: 20 pp.
Subscription fee: Free with membership
Topics: Marine issues, marine mammals, sanctuaries, wildlife
Coverage: Activism, environmental community, organization activities, policy, research
Audience: Citizens, environmental organizations
Scope: Global
Comment: Lots of news about oceans—sanctuaries, endangered species, and pollution.

Ocean and Coastal Law Memo
Ocean and Coastal Law Center
University of Oregon School of Law
Eugene, OR 97403
Phone: 503-346-3845   Fax: 503-346-3985
Richard Hildreth and John Jacobson, Co-Editors
Type: Newsletter
Frequency: 3 issues per year
Length: 8 pp.
Subscription fee: Free

Topics: Environmental law, marine issues, wetlands
Coverage: Legislation
Audience: Professional/academic
Scope: National
Comment: A good source of information about laws and regulations designed to control such marine activities as drift nets, fishery exploitation, and wetland degradation.

Ocean Realm

Raku, Inc.
342 West Sunset Road
San Antonio, TX 78209
Phone: 512-824-8099   Fax: 512-820-3522
Charlene deJori and Cheryl Schorp, Co-Editors
Type: Magazine
Frequency: Quarterly
Length: 104 pp.
Subscription fee: $22
Topics: Marine issues, marine mammals, sanctuaries, wildlife
Coverage: Book reviews, research
Audience: Citizens
Scope: Global
Advertising: Yes
Comment: Mainly about the beauty of the seas, this new glossy magazine includes some news about the various environmental factors assaulting them.

Oceanus

Woods Hole Oceanographic Institution
Woods Hole, MA 02543
Phone: 508-548-1400   Fax: 508-457-2182
Paul R. Ryan, Editor
Type: Journal
Frequency: Quarterly
Length: 100 pp.
Subscription fee: $20
Topics: All marine issues
Coverage: Book reviews, policy, research
Audience: Citizens, professional/academic

Scope: Global
References: Yes
Advertising: Yes
Comment: Engaging, substantive articles, usually written by scientists but accessible to the nonprofessional. Special issues on single topics are common: A recent issue on the Mediterranean includes history of the Mediterranean Sea, its biology and pollution, and a discussion on bouillabaisse.

Sea Grant Abstracts

National Sea Grant Depository
University of Rhode Island
Pell Library Building
Bay Campus
Narragansett, RI 02882
Phone: 401-792-6114
Cynthia Krenicki Murray, Editor
Type: Newsletter
Frequency: Quarterly
Length: 30 pp.
Subscription fee: Free
Topics: Ecosystems, environmental law, fisheries, marine issues
Coverage: Research
Audience: Professional/academic
Scope: Global
Comment: An extremely useful topic-by-topic summary of publications generated by the National Sea Grant College Program.

❖ Organizations

American Cetacean Society
P.O. Box 2639
San Pedro, CA 90731-0943
Phone: 213-548-6279   Fax: 213-548-6950
Patricia Warhol, Executive Director
Purpose: To protect whales and dolphins and the oceans they live in.
Founded: 1967

FYR: 1990
Revenue: Not available
Expenditures: Not available
1990 membership: 3,000
Staff: 3
Chapters: 9
Topics: Conservation, marine mammals, whales
Approaches: Conferences, education, publications, research
Scope: Global
Periodicals: *Whalewatcher* (magazine), *WhaleNews* (newsletter)
Reports: Yes

The American Fisheries Society
5410 Grosvenor Lane
Bethesda, MD 20814
Phone: 301-897-8616   Fax: 301-897-8096
Paul Brouha, Executive Director
Purpose: A professional society dedicated to the advancement of
    fisheries science and the conservation of renewable aquatic
    resources.
Founded: 1870
FYR: 1990
Revenue: $1,972,000
Expenditures: $1,954,000
1990 membership: 9,402
Change from 1989: +4%
Staff: 20
Chapters: 50
Topics: Fisheries, water resources
Approaches: Conferences, education, policy, publications, re-
    search
Scope: International
Periodicals: *Fisheries: A Bulletin of the American Fisheries Society*
    (journal) and several others

American Littoral Society
Sandy Hook
Highlands, NJ 07732
Phone: 908-291-0055

D. W. Bennett, Executive Director
Purpose: To encourage better understanding of the aquatic environment and to advocate protection of the delicate fabric of life along the shore.
Founded: 1961
FYR: 1990
Revenue: [$640,000]
Expenditures: [$640,000]
1990 membership: 9,048
Change from 1989: +9%
Staff: 40
Chapters: 7
Topics: Coastal issues, conservation, habitats, marine issues, recreation
Approaches: Education, publications, research
Scope: International
Special projects: Water Monitoring Program (New Jersey and Staten Island), Volunteer Bay Keeper Program (New Jersey), Fish Tag Program
Periodicals: *Coastal Reporter* (newsletter), *The Underwater Naturalist* (magazine)
Books: Yes
Reports: Yes

Bermuda Biological Station for Research, Inc.
Ferry Reach
GE01
Saint Georges, Bermuda
Phone: 809-297-1880   Fax: 809-297-8143
James N. Galloway, President
Purpose: To offer training and research opportunities for marine scientists worldwide from the special perspective of a mid-ocean island.
Founded: 1926
FYR: 1989
Revenue: $3,140,472
Expenditures: $3,059,970
Staff: 76
Topics: Acid rain, climate change, marine issues, oil spills, sea level change

Approaches: Education, publications, research
Scope: Global
Periodicals: *Currents* (newsletter)

Center for Coastal Studies
59 Commercial Street
Box 1036
Provincetown, MA 02657
Phone: 508-487-3622   Fax: 508-487-4495
Karen L. Steuer, Executive Director
Purpose: To perform research, education, and advisory services
   about the coastal environment.
Founded: 1976
FYR: 1990
Revenue: [$500,000]
Expenditures: [$500,000]
1990 membership: 3,000
Staff: 12
Topics: Entanglement, habitat, marine issues, marine mammals,
   sanctuaries
Approaches: Education, research
Scope: Regional (New England, especially Cape Cod)
Special projects: Population studies of finback and humpback
   whales, Stellwagen Sanctuary, Boston Harbor Cleanup, New
   England Food Web
Periodicals: *Coastwatch* (newsletter)
Books: Yes
Reports: Yes

Center for Marine Conservation
1725 DeSales Street, NW, Suite 500
Washington, DC 20036
Phone: 202-429-5609   Fax: 202-872-0619
Roger E. McManus, President
Purpose: Works broadly to conserve marine habitats and species
   by preserving coastal wetlands, preventing pollution, and
   protecting threatened and endangered species.
Founded: 1972
FYR: 1990

Revenue: $3,603,523
Expenditures: $3,843,797
1990 membership: 110,000
Staff: 35
Chapters: 5
Topics: Biodiversity, coastal issues, ecosystems, endangered species, habitats, marine issues, marine mammals, sanctuaries, whales
Approaches: Advocacy, education, grassroots organizing, litigation, lobbying, publications, research
Scope: Global
Special projects: Florida Keys Sanctuary, International Whaling Coalition
Periodicals: *Marine Conservation News* (newsletter)
Books: Yes

Chesapeake Bay Foundation
162 Prince George Street
Annapolis, MD 21401
Phone: 301-268-8816   Fax: 301-268-6687
William C. Baker, President
Purpose: Taking an ecosystem approach, Chesapeake Bay Foundation works through education, land management, and the law to preserve the Bay watershed.
Founded: 1967
FYR: 1990
Revenue: $5,187,930
Expenditures: $5,364,489
1990 membership: 78,000
Staff: 120
Topics: Coastal issues, fisheries, habitats, hazardous substances, watersheds
Approaches: Advocacy, direct action, education, land acquisition, litigation, publications
Scope: Regional

The Coast Alliance
235 Pennsylvania Avenue, SE
Washington, DC 20003

Phone: 202-546-9554   Fax: 202-546-9609

Beth Millemann, Executive Director

Purpose: A nonprofit public-interest group dedicated to raising public awareness about our priceless coastal resources. Composed of concerned activists across the United States, the Coastal Alliance provides information on activities affecting the nation's coasts.

Founded: 1979

FYR: 1990

Revenue: Not available

Expenditures: Not available

Staff: 3

Topics: Coastal issues, soils, water quality

Approaches: Advocacy, education, grassroots organizing, policy, publications, research

Scope: National

Special projects: Focus on National Flood Insurance Program, Clean Water Act Reauthorization and Contaminated Sediments

Books: Yes

Reports: Yes

Coastal Resources Center

P.O. Box 3084

San Rafael, CA 94912

Phone: 415-788-6150

Stephanie Thornton, Executive Director

Purpose: To conserve the nation's fishery resources and their ecosystems.

Founded: 1985

FYR: 1990

Revenue: [$100,000]

Expenditures: [$90,000]

Staff: 2

Topics: Fisheries, marine issues, ocean dumping, oil spills

Approaches: Conferences, direct action, education, grassroots organizing, publications, research

Scope: National

Special projects: Oil Spill Training and Response, Marine De-

bris Recycling, Fishing Conservation, Matrix of Fisheries Programs and Organizations
Reports: Yes

Cousteau Society, Inc.
930 West 21st Street
Norfolk, VA 23517
Phone: 804-627-1144   Fax: 804-627-7545
Jacques Cousteau, President
Purpose: To protect and improve the quality of life in general, with a primary focus on marine issues.
Founded: 1973
FYR: 1989
Revenue: $14,576,328
Expenditures: $15,726,230
1990 membership: 300,000
Staff: 30
Topics: Conservation, marine issues
Approaches: Education, media, publications, research
Scope: Global
Periodicals: *Calypso Log* (magazine), *The Dolphin Log* (children's magazine)
Reports: Yes

Long Island Sound Taskforce of the Oceanic Society
185 Magee Avenue
Stamford Marine Center
Stamford, CT 06902
Phone: 203-327-9786   Fax: 203-967-2677
Richard Schreiner, Executive Director
Purpose: To promote citizen and government participation in the protection of Long Island Sound.
Founded: 1972
FYR: 1990
Revenue: [$145,000]
Expenditures: [$124,000]
1990 membership: 1,000
Staff: 6
Topics: Marine issues

Approaches: Conferences, education, research
Scope: Regional
Special projects: Citizen Monitoring Program, Information Services (800 Number and Library)
Periodicals: *Long Island Sound Study Update* (newsletter), *On the Sound* (newsletter)

Marine Biological Laboratory
Water Street
Woods Hole, MA 02543
Phone: 508-548-3705   Fax: 508-457-1924
Dr. Harlyn O. Halvorson, Director
Purpose: To provide an international, multi-institutional home for basic biological research and education, as well as a site for coping with the immediate issues of environmental science.
Founded: 1888
FYR: 1990
Revenue: [$17,000,000]
Expenditures: [$17,000,000]
1990 membership: 750
Staff: 212
Topics: Basic research, biomedical sciences, marine issues
Approaches: Advocacy, conferences, education, funding, publications, research
Scope: Global
Special projects: Marine Resources Center and the Advanced Studies Laboratory (both are part of the Marine Biomedical Institute for Advanced Studies)
Periodicals: *LabNotes 91* (newsletter), *The Collecting Net* (newsletter), *MBL Science* (journal)
Reports: Yes

Marine Policy Center
Woods Hole Oceanographic Institute (WHOI)
Woods Hole, MA 02543
Phone: 508-548-1400   Fax: 508-548-1400
James M. Broadus, Director
Purpose: To perform social science and policy studies for

WHOI. Resident staff and research fellows study such topics as the economics of ocean space and the role of science in government and industry decisions.
Founded: 1971
FYR: 1990
Revenue: [$1,600,000]
Expenditures: [$1,200,000]
Staff: 27
Topics: International security, marine issues
Approaches: Conferences, education, policy, publications, research
Scope: Global
Special projects: Environmental Security and the World Oceans: Analytic Approaches and Shared Solutions

National Aquarium in Baltimore
Pier 3
501 East Pratt Street
Baltimore, MD 21202
Phone: 301-576-3874   Fax: 301-576-8238
Nicholas Brown, Executive Director
Purpose: A wonderful facility designed to educate the public about our ocean planet and why marine habitats should be preserved. Special focus on marine mammals.
Founded: 1981
FYR: 1990
Revenue: [$20,642,725]
Expenditures: [$20,642,725]
Staff: 240
Topics: Biodiversity, endangered species, marine issues, whales
Approaches: Education, publications, research
Scope: National
Periodicals: *Watermarks* (newsletter)
Reports: Yes

National Coalition for Marine Conservation, Inc.
P.O. Box 23298
Savannah, GA 31403

Phone: 912-234-8062   Fax: 912-233-2909
Ken Hinman, Executive Director
Purpose: To stop the destruction of America's ocean fisheries and promote public awareness of the conservation ethic.
Founded: 1973
FYR: 1989
Revenue: $88,866
Expenditures: 82,563
1990 membership: 1,000
Staff: 2
Topics: Conservation, fisheries, marine issues
Approaches: Conferences, publications
Scope: National
Special projects: Annual Symposium
Periodicals: *Currents* (newsletter), *Marine Bulletin* (newsletter), *Ocean View* (newsletter)
Reports: Yes

National Fish and Wildlife Foundation
18th and C Street, NW, Room 2556
Washington, DC 20240
Phone: 202-208-3040   Fax: 202-208-4051
Charles H. Collins, Executive Director
Purpose: Set up by Congress to encourage, accept and administer private gifts and property that enhance the activities of the U.S. Fish and Wildlife Service.
Founded: 1984
FYR: 1990
Revenue: $8,257,403
Expenditures: $6,612,082
Staff: 15
Topics: Ecosystems, endangered species, fisheries, marine issues, wildlife
Approaches: Education, funding, land acquisition, publications, research
Scope: National
Periodicals: *Federal Agency Needs Assessment* (annual)
Books: Yes

Sea Shepherd Conservation Society
1314 Second Street
Santa Monica, CA 90401
Phone: 213-394-3198   Fax: 213-378-4282
Paul Watson, Director
Purpose: Taking the activist approach to marine wildlife conservation, Sea Shepherd polices the oceans in an attempt to stop the illegal slaughter of marine mammals.
Founded: 1977
FYR: 1990
Revenue: $614,173
Expenditures: $523,243
1990 membership: 15,000
Change from 1989: +30%
Staff: 3
Chapters: 2
Affiliates: Earth First!, Earth Island Institute, Fund for Animals
Topics: Endangered species, fisheries, marine issues, especially marine mammals
Approaches: Advocacy, direct action, education, grassroots organizing
Scope: Global
Special projects: Drift nets, Dolphin Protection, Icelandic Whaling
Periodicals: *Sea Shepherd Log* (newsletter)
Books: Yes

Tarlton Foundation
1160 Battery Street, Suite 360
San Francisco, CA 94111
Phone: 415-433-3163   Fax: 415-989-7867
Margaret Elliott, Director
Purpose: Formerly the Ocean Alliance, this newly reorganized group works to fight pollution and promote conservation of the oceans.
Founded: 1991 (reorganization)
FYR: 1990
Revenue: Not available
Expenditures: Not available

Staff: 6
Topics: Marine issues
Approaches: Advocacy, conservation, education, research
Scope: Global

Woods Hole Oceanographic Institution (WHOI)

Woods Hole, MA 02543
Phone: 508-548-1400
John H. Steele, Director
Purpose: To perform oceanographic research. WHOI has about 350 projects under way at any one time on a wide range of marine science topics.
Founded: 1930
FYR: 1990
Revenue: $70,000,000
Expenditures: $70,000,000
1990 membership: 1,500
Staff: 1,000
Affiliates: Center for Marine Policy, Center for Marine Exploration, Coastal Research Center
Topics: Coastal issues, marine issues, oceanography
Approaches: Conferences, education, publications, research
Scope: Global
Periodicals: *Oceanus* (journal)
Reports: Yes

❑ Foundation Funding

In 1990, about 7 percent of the dollars awarded by U.S. independent and community foundations for environmental purposes went for marine projects.

❑   **ENVIRONMENTAL GRANT-MAKING FOUNDATIONS:**   ❑
FUNDING FOR MARINE PROJECTS, 1990

Rank	Foundation	Number of Grants	Dollars Awarded
1	The David and Lucille Packard Foundation	4	7,607,000
2	The Atlantic Foundation	1	2,800,000
3	Mary Flagler Cary Charitable Foundation	12	1,470,000
4	The Andrew W. Mellon Foundation	2	500,000
5	The William and Flora Hewlett Foundation	3	455,000
6	The Educational Foundation of America	4	431,762
7	Chesapeake Bay Trust	20	384,849
8	The Pew Charitable Trusts	2	345,000
9	The San Francisco Foundation	14	344,700
10	The New Hampshire Charitable Fund	6	244,062

9

Solid Waste

THE UNITED STATES GENERATES about 10 billion metric tons of nonagricultural solid waste every year. Municipal solid waste accounts for only a tiny fraction (1.5 percent) of this, but adds up to more than 150 million metric tons, costing between $4 billion and $5 billion to dispose of each year. The average U.S. citizen discards between three and six pounds of waste every day.

We should perhaps be more concerned with the bigger sources of waste: industry, mining, forestry, and agriculture. But citizen-generated waste deserves our attention for three reasons: (1) unlike the waste generated from other sources, municipal solid waste cannot be left where it's made—it has to be taken somewhere else for disposal; (2) we discard it ourselves, so it seems more directly our responsibility; and (3) as its quantities grow, the number of places to put it are dwindling.

Most municipal solid waste in our country consists of paper and paper products (35.6 percent). Yard wastes are second (20.1 percent), followed by roughly equal amounts of food, metals, plastics, and glass (7 to 9 percent each), then smaller amounts of textiles, rubber, and wood. Packaging accounts for a huge share of the household trash heap: 30 percent by weight, 50 percent by volume.

There are only four ways to deal with solid waste: dump it, burn it, convert it into something that can be used again, or don't make it. At present, 73 percent of these wastes are dumped, 14 percent incinerated, and 13 percent recycled. Very little effort is made to discourage the production that makes waste possible.

LANDFILLS. Dumping waste on land is the conventional method of waste disposal. Dumps were sited just about anywhere until passage of the first federal statute, the Resource Conservation and Recovery Act (RCRA) of 1976. As newly amended, RCRA-requires that landfill owners comply with strict provisions for siting, housekeeping, and monitoring landfill wastewater and airborne emissions. But landfills still have their problems:

- Most landfills contain hazardous wastes; at present, many contaminate groundwater and release methane gas. In addition, recent research has unearthed a major problem with landfill disposal: Concealed from light and air, even organic matter will not biodegrade.

- As operation becomes more costly and regulations more stringent, landfills are closing. Of the 18,000 landfills operating in 1976, half had closed by 1989, and only 6,000 are expected to remain open through 1993. According to EPA estimates, only 1,800 will be operating by 2010.

INCINERATION. The second most common means of disposal, incineration has been touted as the solution to the waste problem. In 1989, there were 50 incinerators and 122 waste-to-energy (WTE) facilities operating nationwide; 31 WTE facilities were under construction and 74 under contract. By April 1991 136 WTE facilities were in operation, handling about 16 percent of the solid waste stream.

Incineration reduces waste 70 percent by volume and it is increasingly used to generate energy. However:

- Facilities cost up to $400 million apiece and deteriorate rapidly.

- Incineration creates air pollution (including toxic emissions such as acid gases, heavy metals, dioxins, and furans).

- Incineration creates huge quantities of ash that then need disposal, usually in a landfill. This ash contains toxic residues. Despite legal challenges, the EPA has not classified incinerator ash as hazardous waste on the grounds that disposal costs would be too great.

- More energy can be saved by recycling most items than can be produced by burning them.

Under the 1990 Clean Air Act, the EPA is required to regulate incinerators. In 1991 the EPA proposed regulations that included mandated recycling and the removal of certain hazardous substances such as lead batteries from the waste stream before incineration. These regulations were designed to reduce the toxicity of incinerator emissions and ash. But they have been delayed and weakened by business interests and the Bush administration, who argue they will increase the already high cost of incineration. It is not clear when—and in what form—the regulations will be promulgated.

Recycling. Besides reducing waste, recycling lowers the demand for energy, water, and raw materials. It also lowers the potential for air and water pollution.

Environmental Benefits of Recycling, by Material

REDUCTION OF:	PERCENT REDUCTION IF RECYCLED			
	ALUMINUM	STEEL	PAPER	GLASS
Energy Use	90–97	47–74	23–74	4–32
Air Pollution	95	85	75	20
Water Pollution	97	76	35	—
Mining Wastes	—	97	—	80
Water Use	—	40	58	50

Source: Robert Cowles Letcher and Mary T. Scheil, "Source Separation and Citizen Recycling," in William D. Robinson, ed. *The Solid Waste Handbook* (New York: Wiley, 1986).

As the dimensions of the waste crisis have become clearer, U.S. citizens have responded to the concept of recycling with unanticipated enthusiasm. As of 1991, 11 percent of municipal solid waste was being recycled; the nationwide target for 1992 was 25 percent, and a number of municipalities and counties had already exceeded that target. In 1989, 23 percent of paper, 9 percent of glass, and 25 percent of aluminum products were being recycled nationwide. Recycling programs for other metals, plastics, and yard wastes have not yet been as successful. And overall we have not begun to approach the success rate of Japan, which recycles or reuses 50 percent of its solid waste, sending only 27 percent to landfills.

The most critical factor for recycling today is creation of the infrastructure (markets for used and recycled materials). Without strong markets to ensure economic viability, recycling cannot succeed. The "green" movement in the United States, considerably boosted by Earth Day 1990, has certainly helped create markets for recyclables. Whether these and other markets for recycled goods will be viable without tax incentives and other kinds of governmental support is still unclear.

Many barriers to recycling still exist within our economy. The Recycling Advisory Committee was recently created to help overcome these barriers through consensus-building between industry, government, and citizens. It was established by the National Recycling Coalition and is partially funded by a three-year EPA grant. Some of the issues the Committee has highlighted include the need for national labeling and marketing programs, standards and definitions for recycled products, and design for recyclability. The committee is also examining federal subsidies for virgin fibers such as timber from the national forests, which compete with recycled fibers in the marketplace.

COMPOSTING. Approximately 70 percent of the U.S. municipal waste stream is compostable. Composting returns waste materials to the Earth the way natural systems do. But it should not be regarded as a substitute for separating and recycling waste, nor as an excuse to continue producing disposable products.

Many states have banned yard wastes from landfills, placing the burden on local governments to organize and implement yard wastes composting projects. These projects are proceeding quite successfully. Now, attention is turning toward mixed waste composting, a relatively new technology. In order for mixed waste composting to be successful, recyclable, hazardous, and inorganic materials must be removed from the waste before it is composted. Odors must be controlled, and the finished project must meet strict standards for both physical and chemical quality.

SOURCE REDUCTION. Despite all the news about the trash crisis, garbage mountains, and waste-laden ships without a port, municipal solid waste continues to grow at a rate of 1 to 2 percent a year. A small part of the increase can be attributed to population growth, but the rest comes from a continuing growth in per capita waste generation. Because all other strategies are essentially magic tricks (transforming waste from one medium to another), source reduction must be our real goal. Source reduction, as a first step, involves such things as packaging reform, conversion to reusable linens and dishware, and double-sided copying.

Just as in the case of energy, the real waste problem is overconsumption by the world's more fortunate populations, described in the Worldwatch Institute's *State of the World 1991* as "an environmental problem unmatched in severity by anything but perhaps population growth." Measured in constant dollars, the world's people have consumed as many goods and services since 1950 as all previous generations have consumed throughout human history.

Most of the consumption thus far has occurred in the more developed countries of the North. But the problem knows no geographic bounds and seems to accompany development and increasing gross national product.

In the final analysis, no matter how well we deal with the stuff we throw away, continuing to throw it away is no solution at all. To truly resolve the waste problem, we will have to design a new kind of society, where ever-increasing production and consumption are no longer considered positive goals.

RESOURCES

☙ Books and Reports

America's Waste: Managing for Risk Reduction. Washington, DC: The Conservation Foundation. 1987, 81 pp.

Approaches to Source Reduction: Practical Guidance from Existing Policies and Programs. Berkeley, CA: The Environmental Defense Fund. June 1986, 148 pp.

Beyond the Crisis: Integrated Solid Waste Management. Santa Barbara, CA: Community Environmental Council, Inc. 1990, 43 pp.

Cleaning Up: U.S. Waste Management Technology and Third World Development. John Elkington and Jonathan Shapley. Washington, DC: World Resources Institute. 1985, 92 pp.

Coming Full Circle: Successful Recycling Today. New York: Environmental Defense Fund. 1988, 162 pp.

Curbing Waste in a Throwaway World: Report of the Task Force on Solid Waste Management. Washington, DC: National Governors Association. 1990, 68 pp.

Discarding the Throwaway Society. Worldwatch Paper 101. John E. Young. Washington, DC: Worldwatch Institute. 1991, 45 pp.

"Fact Packets" issued by the Solid Waste Alternatives Project (SWAP) of the Environmental Action Foundation:

- Composting Fact Packet
- Degradable Plastics: The "Feel Good" Solution to the Plastics Disposal Dilemma
- Disposable Diapers
- Source Reduction
- Incineration

Washington, DC: Environmental Action Foundation. 1989–91.

From Pollution to Prevention: A Progress Report on Waste. Washington, DC: Office of Technology Assessment. 1987, 54 pp.

Garbage Management in Japan: Leading the Way. Allen Hershkowitz and Eugene Salerni. New York: INFORM. 1987, 131 pp.

Getting at the Source: Strategies for Reducing Municipal Solid Waste. World Wildife Fund. Washington, DC: Island Press. June 1992, 138 pp.

Household Waste: Issues and Opportunities. Washington, DC: Concern, Inc. 1989, 30 pp.

Taking out the Trash: A No-Nonsense Guide to Recycling. Jennifer Carless. Washington, DC: Island Press. June 1992, 300 pp.

Waste: Choices for Communities. Washington, DC: Concern, Inc. 1988, 30 pp.

Yard Waste Composting: A Study of Eight Programs. Washington, DC: U.S. Environmental Protection Agency. April 1989, 47 pp.

❂ Periodicals

BioCycle: Journal of Waste Recycling
J. G. Press, Inc.
Box 351
18 South 17th Street
Emmaus, PA 18049
Phone: 215-967-4135
Jerome Goldstein, Editor

Type: Journal
Frequency: Monthly
Length: 86 pp.
Subscription fee: $55
Topics: Composting, recycling, solid waste
Coverage: Organization activities, research
Audience: Business/industry
Scope: International
Advertising: Yes
Comment: A somewhat technical journal on recycling for professionals and citizens who have a deep interest in the solid waste crisis.

Garbage

Old-House Journal Corporation
435 Ninth Street
Brooklyn, NY 11215
Phone: 718-788-1700   Fax: 718-788-9051
Patricia Poore, Editor
Type: Magazine
Frequency: Bimonthly
Length: 60 pp.
Subscription fee: $21
Topics: Environmental/occupational health, hazardous waste, incineration, industry, recycling, solid waste
Coverage: Organization activities, research
Audience: Citizens
Scope: National
Advertising: Yes
Comment: An attractive and highly successful new periodical that tells a lot about garbage and much more—recently exploring issues such as population, water resources, natural gardens, and big industry.

Plastics Recycling Update

Resource Recycling, Inc.
P.O. Box 10540
Portland, OR 97210
Phone: 503-227-1319   Fax: 503-227-3864

Jerry Powell, Editor
Type: Newsletter
Frequency: Monthly
Length: 6 pp.
Subscription fee: $85
Topics: Recycling
Coverage: Business/industry
Audience: Business/industry
Scope: National
Comment: A readable newsbrief about plastics recycling pro-
    grams and markets.

Recycling Times
National Solid Waste Management Association
1730 Rhode Island Avenue, NW, Suite 1000
Washington, DC 20036
Phone: 202-861-0708   Fax: 202-775-5917
Joseph A. Salimando, Editor
Type: Newsletter
Frequency: Biweekly
Length: 16 pp.
Subscription fee: $95
Topics: Recycling, incentives, markets, solid waste
Coverage: Business/industry, organization activities, research
Audience: Business/industry
Scope: National
Advertising: Yes
Comment: The best source we've found for up-to-date informa-
    tion on recycling markets nationwide.

Resource Recovery Report
Resource Recovery Report
5313 38th Street, NW
Washington, DC 20015
Phone: 202-362-6034   Fax: 202-362-6632
Frank McManus, Editor
Type: Newsletter
Frequency: Monthly
Length: 10 pp.

Subscription fee: $177
Topics: Recycling, solid waste
Coverage: Business/industry
Audience: Citizens, government
Scope: National
Comment: This newsletter has no index, but seems to give bits and pieces of news about (1) federal events; (2) innovative projects around the country; (3) specific components of trash; and (4) the states. Useful to skim, but could be better organized.

Resource Recycling

Resource Recycling, Inc.
P.O. Box 10540
Portland, OR 97210
Phone: 503-227-1319   Fax: 503-227-3864
Jerry Powell, Editor
Type: Journal
Frequency: Monthly
Length: 100 pp.
Subscription fee: $42
Topics: Recycling, solid waste
Coverage: Business/industry, organization activities
Audience: Business/industry, government
Scope: National
Advertising: Yes
Comment: This monthly documents many facets of the rapidly growing field of recycling, including markets, trends, and state and national policy.

Waste Age

National Solid Wastes Management Association
1730 Rhode Island Avenue, NW, Suite 1000
Washington, DC 20036
Phone: 202-659-4613
John T. Aquino, Editor
Type: Magazine
Frequency: Monthly
Length: 170 pp.

Subscription fee: $45
Topics: Composting, incineration, landfills, markets, recycling, solid waste
Coverage: Business/industry, research
Audience: Business/industry, citizens, government
Scope: National
Advertising: Yes
Comment: A complete and authoritative source, geared towards professionals but indispensable for citizens who want to be informed about all facets of solid waste management.

❖ Organizations

Central States Resource Center
809 S. Fifth Street
Champaign, IL 61820
Phone: 217-344-2371   Fax: 217-344-2371
John Thompson, Executive Director
Purpose: To provide technical and organizing assistance to grassroots environmental organizations.
Founded: 1968
FYR: 1989
Revenue: $98,519
Expenditures: $103,064
1990 membership: 400
Staff: 6
Topics: Incineration, landfills, low-level nuclear waste, solid waste, source reduction
Approaches: Grassroots organizing
Scope: Regional (primarily Illinois and Indiana)
Special projects: Model Community Program
Periodicals: *Central States Bulletin* (newsletter)
Books: Yes
Reports: Yes

Citizens for a Better Environment
33 E. Congress Street, Suite 523
Chicago, IL 60605

Phone: 312-939-1530
William Davis, Regional Director
Purpose: To resolve local and regional environmental problems. Current emphases are toxics use reduction and solid waste.
Founded: 1971
FYR: 1990
Revenue: [$1,500,000]
Expenditures: [$1,500,000]
1990 membership: 30,000
Staff: 20
Chapters: 3
Topics: Hazardous substances and waste, solid waste, source reduction, water quality
Approaches: Advocacy, grassroots organizing
Scope: Regional
Special projects: Toxics Use Reduction
Periodicals: *Environmental Review* (fact sheets)

Community Environmental Council, Inc.
930 Miramonte Drive
Santa Barbara, CA 93109
Phone: 805-963-0583   Fax: 805-962-9080
John Clark, Executive Director
Purpose: To collect and distribute information about environmental and related issues. The Council operates the Gildea Research Center, three community gardens, and several recycling centers in Santa Barbara County.
Founded: 1970
FYR: 1990
Revenue: [$4,000,000]
Expenditures: [$4,000,000]
1990 Membership: 750
Staff: 70
Topics: Hazardous waste, recycling and source reduction, sustainable agriculture, sustainable cities
Approaches: Conferences, dispute resolution, education, grassroots organizing, internships, law/policy, publications, research
Scope: National

Special projects: Curbside recycling, hazardous waste collection in Santa Barbara
Periodicals: *Gildea Review* (newsletter)
Books: Yes
Reports: Yes

INFORM, Inc.
381 Park Avenue South, Suite 1201
New York, NY 10016
Phone: 212-689-4040
Joanna D. Underwood, President
Purpose: Although it deals with more than waste, INFORM has done a lot on this issue. INFORM works to identify practical ways to protect our natural resources and public health.
Founded: 1974
FYR: 1990
Revenue: $1,310,000
Expenditures: $1,270,000
1990 membership: 1,000
Staff: 30
Topics: All environmental, but especially agricultural irrigation, air pollution, recycling, solid waste, and water use
Approaches: Education, publications, research
Scope: National
Special projects: *The Business Recycling Manual*
Periodicals: *INFORM Reports* (newsletter)
Books: Yes
Reports: Yes

Keep America Beautiful, Inc.
Mill River Plaza
9 West Broad Street
Stamford, CT 06902
Phone: 203-323-8987   Fax: 203-325-9199
Roger W. Powers, President
Purpose: Sponsored primarily by industry, this organization works to improve waste-handling practices on the community level.
Founded: 1953
FYR: 1990

Revenue: [$1,900,000]
Expenditures: [$1,900,000]
Staff: 19
Affiliates: 471 affiliates
Topics: Beautification, litter, solid waste
Approaches: Education
Scope: National
Special projects: Public Lands Stewardship Program
Periodicals: *Vision* (newsletter)
Reports: Yes

Minnesota Project
1885 University Avenue W, Suite 315
St. Paul, MN 55104
Phone: 612-645-6159
Beth E. Waterhouse, Executive Director
Purpose: To work with rural communities as they build their
    capacity to solve their own development and resource man-
    agement problems. Major program areas are groundwater
    protection, sustainable agriculture, alternative solid waste
    management, and community-based development.
Founded: 1979
FYR: 1990
Revenue: $479,194
Expenditures: $441,147
Staff: 8
Chapters: 2
Topics: Groundwater protection, hazardous waste management,
    leadership development, market development for recycled
    materials, rural recycling, sustainable agriculture, water re-
    duction, water planning
Approaches: Advocacy, conferences, eduction, grassroots orga-
    nizing, law/policy, publications, research
Scope: Regional
Books: Yes
Reports: Yes

National Recycling Coalition
1101 30th Street, NW
Washington, DC 20007

Phone: 202-625-6406   Fax: 202-625-6409
David Loveland, Executive Director
Purpose: Education, technical assistance, and public policy to promote effective recycling programs.
Founded: 1978
FYR: 1990
Revenue: Not available
Expenditures: Not available
1990 membership: 3,500
% change: +15%
Staff: 10
Chapters: 27
Topics: Recycling
Approaches: Advocacy, conferences, education, law/policy, publications, research
Scope: International
Special projects: Buy Recycled, National Recycling Advisory Council
Periodicals: *Connection* (newsletter)
Reports: Yes

National Solid Wastes Management Association

1730 Rhode Island Avenue, NW, Suite 1000
Washington, DC 20036
Phone: 202-659-4613
Eugene J. Wingerter, Executive Director
Purpose: A trade group representing the private waste services industry, the association also "serves as an advocate for state and federal laws that will preserve our country's natural resources while allowing local communities to address their growing waste management needs."
Founded: 1968
FYR: 1990
Revenue: Not available
Expenditures: Not available
1990 Membership: 2,500 companies
Staff: 107
Chapters: 31
Topics: Industry, hazardous waste, landfill, medical waste, recycling, resource recovery, waste-to-energy.

Approaches: Advocacy, conferences, education, law/policy, lob-
bying, publications, research
Scope: International
Special projects: Waste Expo (annual convention and trade
show), regional seminars and workshops, *Recycling in the
States: 1990 Review*
Periodicals: *Waste Age* (magazine), *Recycling Times* (newsletter)
Books: Yes
Reports: Yes

❏ Foundation Funding

In 1990, about 2 percent of the dollars awarded by U.S. independent and community foundations for environmental programs went for solid waste projects.

❏   ENVIRONMENTAL GRANT-MAKING FOUNDATIONS: ❏
FUNDING FOR SOLID WASTE PROJECTS, 1990

Rank	Foundation	Number of Grants	Dollars Awarded
1	The Chicago Community Trust	17	710,000
2	The Pew Charitable Trusts	3	340,000
3	Joyce Mertz-Gilmore Foundation	5	310,000
4	Rockefeller Brothers Fund	1	300,000
5	The Ford Foundation	2	255,000
6	Waste Management, Inc.	9	227,000
7	Z. Smith Reynolds Foundation, Inc.	6	158,000
8	Mary Reynolds Babcock Foundation, Inc.	4	140,000
9	W. Alton Jones Foundation, Inc.	5	115,900
10	North Shore Unitarian Universalist Veatch Program	3	100,000
11	Robert Sterling Clark Foundation, Inc.	2	100,000

10

Hazardous Substances And Waste

CONCERN ABOUT HAZARDOUS SUB-
stances (often referred to as "toxics") and their disposal arose
in the late 1970s when chemicals at the abandoned Love Canal
dump site were found to be contaminating soils and groundwater beneath the houses built on the site. Since then, "toxics"
has become an issue with high visibility within the environmental movement.

The toxics problem has several components:

- Industry produces huge quantities of chemicals. The
  toxicity of most of these chemicals is unknown.

- Disposal of many industrial chemicals has historically
  been indiscriminate and unregulated.

- Exposure to industrial dump sites and effluent tends to
  be greatest among the poor and minority groups.

- A patchwork of regulations now governs hazardous waste production and disposal. The system is cumbersome at best.

- Hazardous waste cleanup, now mandated by law, is an extremely costly and time-consuming process.

- The basic problem is how to achieve source reduction.

TOXIC CHEMICAL PRODUCTION

Toxic chemicals are substances harmful to living organisms. Some may be harmful only to some plants or some animals but not to humans. Others may be harmful to humans and not to other species. Toxic chemicals may be natural or of human origin.

A wide range of human activities entails toxic chemical production or use. They include agriculture, energy production, mining, manufacturing, transportation, and household activities.

An enormous volume of chemicals is produced today. Production of synthetic organic chemicals in the United States grew fifteenfold from 1945 to 1986, from 6.7 million to 102 million metric tons. Worldwide, 70,000 chemicals are in everyday use, and between 500 and 1,000 new chemicals are added to commercial production every year. In the United States, we regularly use more than 62,000 chemicals in industry, agriculture, and medicine.

Little is known about how most of these chemicals affect human health or the environment. The EPA lists about 50,000 toxic substances, but has toxicity information on less than 80 percent. Much of that information is sketchy; it rarely includes data drawn from human studies.

HAZARDOUS WASTE DISPOSAL

No one knows just how much hazardous waste is produced in the United States each year. Estimates have ranged from 264 million tons (EPA) to 400 million tons (Office of Technology Assessment). One very recent estimate is provided by the relatively new Toxics Release Inventory (TRI). Mandated by 1987 amendments to the Superfund Act, TRI is an annual compilation of information on the release of 332 toxic chemicals by manufacturing facilities with more than ten employees.

In 1989, the third year of TRI reporting, a total of 22,650 manufacturers reported releasing 5.7 billion pounds of toxic chemicals into the air, land, and water. Of this total, 2.4 billion pounds were released into air; 1.2 billion pounds into underground injection wells; 189 million pounds into rivers, lakes, and streams; and 445 million pounds into landfills.

Although the TRI gives us better data than have ever before been available, environmentalists tend to question its accuracy. In 1991 a coalition of environmental groups led by the Natural Resources Defense Council asserted that 95 percent of toxic releases are unaccounted for in the TRI because of noncompliance, low estimates, and limitations on the number of chemicals and facilities subject to reporting requirements.

A report by the U.S. Public Interest Research Group estimates that 350 billion pounds of toxic chemicals (equal to 1,400 pounds for each U.S. citizen) are actually produced and used in the United States each year. The study found three states— Louisiana, Texas, and Ohio—each producing between 10 billion and 100 billion pounds.

Although we don't know the exact quantities involved, we do know that the vast majority of hazardous waste is disposed of on or near the site where it is produced. Only about 5 percent gets shipped off-site to landfills, incinerators, or foreign ports. With increasingly strict regulations, landfill now costs more than $250 a ton and incineration costs $500 to $1200 a ton. As a result, U.S. companies export upwards of 160,000 tons of hazardous waste a year. Most goes to Canada and Mexico, but some goes to the very poorest developing countries, which accept it to generate revenue, but which certainly cannot afford safe disposal.

In March 1989, the United States signed the Basel Convention on the Control of Transboundary Movements of Hazardous Wastes and Their Disposal. Originally intended to ban the international trade in hazardous wastes, this United Nations treaty in its final form in fact legitimizes it, allowing export with consent from the recipient.

In May 1991, the Bush administration sent the Hazardous and Additional Waste Export and Import Act of 1991 to Congress, asking for ratification of the Basel Convention. The Basel Convention has now been signed by 54 countries and ratified by 10. It is expected to come into force by the spring of 1992, when it has been ratified by 20 nations.

The proposed plan would, however, apply to less than 10 percent of the hazardous waste currently exported from the United States. It would not affect commerce between the United States, Canada, and Mexico, which accounts for over 90 percent of our hazardous waste exports. It would exclude shipments of scrap metals and textiles, waste paper, glass, and plastics when they are exported for recycling. It would also exclude radioactive wastes.

REGULATION

Within the United States, toxic chemicals are regulated under various federal statutes rather than through a single coherent scheme. Some of the most important measures are:

- The Toxic Substances Control Act (TSCA) and the Federal Insecticide, Fungicide and Rodenticide Act (FIFRA). Both deal with chemical production and commerce.

- The Resource Conservation and Recovery Act (RCRA), the Clean Air Act, and the Clean Water Act. These regulate ongoing chemical discharges.

- The Comprehensive Environmental Response, Compensation, and Liability Act (CERCLA, commonly known as Superfund). Enacted in December 1980, Superfund provided for emergency response and for the identification and cleanup of the most hazardous closed and abandoned waste sites. Amendments to CERCLA (known as SARA) deal with hazardous discharge. The Toxics Release Inventory falls under Section 313 of the Emergency Planning and Community Right-to-Know Act of SARA.

CLEANUP

Superfund has become a highly controversial part of our national environmental policy. The complex administrative and legal steps required to select sites for cleanup and to hold owners, transporters, and dumpers financially responsible have proved difficult to carry out. The whole process is inordinately slow and very expensive. For example:

- Between 1980 and 1988, 1,193 of 30,000 proposed sites made the National Priorities List for cleanup. By the end of 1988, plans had been approved for 433 sites; remediation was under way at 177, but cleanup had been completed at only 32 sites. As of February 1991, 1,189 sites were on the list.

- By the end of 1988, $5 billion had been spent under Superfund. The congressional Office of Technology Assessment (OTA) estimates that expenditures may eventually top $100 billion as the list grows, perhaps ultimately to include some 10,000 sites.

Despite its problems, Superfund has a positive side. The provisions of the law that hold landowners responsible for waste on their property, even if they did not dump it there, have had interesting consequences. Major land purchasers now routinely check for spills or dumping and many financial institutions require such investigations before making loans for property purchase or development.

SOURCE REDUCTION

In the 1984 amendments to RCRA, waste minimization became federal policy: "Wherever feasible, the generation of hazardous waste is to be reduced or eliminated as expeditiously as possible." The EPA estimates that expanded use of existing technologies alone could cut total U.S. industrial hazardous waste by 15 to 30 percent.

Yet, according to the OTA, the federal government has given ambiguous signals to industry about the need for waste minimization by encouraging waste treatment and disposal. And although the EPA created an Office of Waste Minimization in 1987, federal expenditures for waste minimization have remained modest.

Responding to federal inaction, the states have taken the lead. In 1987, the Council of State Governments (CSG), a national organization of the fifty states, developed model state legislation to reduce hazardous waste. A number of states, including California, Illinois, Minnesota, New York, Pennsylvania, Texas, and Wisconsin, now have aggressive strategies for waste reduction.

One of the best publicized programs to date is North Carolina's Pollution Prevention Pays. With an annual budget of $600,000, it gives technical assistance, research, and education, and makes matching grants to help business and communities implement waste reduction and recycling plans.

In February 1991, the EPA unveiled a new strategy for pollution prevention: a voluntary program called the Industrial Toxics Project (ITP) or the "33-50" initiative. This plan asks industry to cut its emissions of 17 chemicals included in the Toxics Release Inventory by one-third of the 1988 level before the end of 1992, and by one-half before the end of 1995. To announce this plan, the EPA sent letters to the top 600 chemical companies reporting releases of these chemicals. As of May 1991, 200 companies had expressed an interest in the program.

The concept for the Industrial Toxics Project stems from the EPA Science Advisory Board's September 1990 report, *Reducing Risk: Setting Priorities and Strategies for Environmental Protection*, which recommended:

- An emphasis on pollution prevention;

- An increased reliance on information tools such as the TRI instead of command and control;

- An integrated, multimedia approach to environmental problems; and

- An identification of toxic chemicals as among the most serious concerns.

Toxics represents only one of the several sectors targeted by the EPA. The others are agriculture, energy, transportation, and federal facilities. It will be interesting to observe whether the Bush administration's strategy can make headway with the toxics problem.

RESOURCES

☞ Books and Reports

Alternatives to Landfilling Household Toxics. Sacramento, CA: Golden Empire Health Planning Center. 1987, 196 pp.

America's Future in Toxic Waste Management. Bruce W. Piasecki and Gary A. Davis. New York: Quorum Books. 1987, 325 pp.

Citizen's Toxic Protection Manual. Boston: The National Toxics Campaign. 1988, 560 pp.

Cutting Chemical Wastes. New York: INFORM. 1986, 528 pp.

Defusing the Toxics Threat: Controlling Pesticides and Industrial Waste. Worldwatch Paper 79. Sandra Postel. Washington, DC: Worldwatch Institute. September 1987, 69 pp.

The Dynamic Duo: RCRA and SARA Title III. Carol Dansereau. Washington, DC: Environmental Action Foundation. June 1989, 57 pp.

Everyday Chemicals: 101 Practical Tips for Home and Work. Beth Richman and Susan Hassol. Snowmass, CO: The Windstar Foundation. 1989, 68 pp.

Fighting Toxics: A Manual for Protecting Your Family, Community, and Workplace. Gary Cohen and John O'Connor, editors. National Toxics Campaign. Washington, DC: Island Press. 1990, 346 pp.

High Tech and Toxics: A Guide for Local Communities. Susan Sherry. Sacramento, CA: Golden Empire Health Planning Center. 1985, 465 pp.

An Ounce of Toxic Pollution Prevention: Rating States' Toxics Use Reduction Laws. William Ryan and Richard Shrader. Washington, DC: National Environmental Law Center and Center for Policy Alternatives. 1991, 22 pp.

Regulating Pesticides in Food: The Delaney Paradox. Washington, DC: National Academy Press. 1987, 272 pp.

The Right to Know More. New York: Natural Resources Defense Council. 1991, 71 pp.

The Risk Assessment of Environmental Hazards: A Textbook of Case Studies. Dennis J. Pausenbach, editor. New York: John Wiley & Sons. 1989, 1155 pp.

Risk Management and Hazardous Waste: Implementation and the Dialectics of Credibility. Brian Wynne. Berlin: Springer-Verlag. 1987, 444 pp.

Serious Reduction of Hazardous Waste: For Pollution Prevention and Industrial Efficiency. U.S. Congress, Office of Technology Assessment. Washington, DC: National Technical Information Service. 1986, 264 pp.

Toxic Chemicals, Health, and the Environment. Lester B. Lave and Arthur C. Upton. Baltimore: Johns Hopkins University Press. 1987, 304 pp.

Toxic Truth and Consequences. Washington, DC: U.S. Public Interest Research Group. April 1991, 36 pp.

Toxics in the Air: Reassessing the Regulatory Framework. Washington, DC: The Conservation Foundation. 1987, 62 pp.

The Toxics-Release Inventory: A National Perspective, 1989. United States Environmental Protection Agency. June 1991, 374 pp.

Trash into Cash: Waste Management Inc.'s Environmental Crimes & Misdeeds. Washington, DC: Greenpeace USA. 1991, 37 pp.

Understanding Superfund: A Progress Report. Jan Paul Acton. Santa Monica, CA: RAND. 1989, 65 pp.

❂ Periodicals

Everyone's Backyard
Citizens Clearinghouse for Hazardous Wastes
P.O. Box 926
Arlington, VA 22216
Phone: 703-276-7070
Will Collette, Editor
Type: Newsletter
Frequency: Bimonthly
Length: 30 pp.
Subscription fee: Free with membership
Topics: Hazardous substances and waste, solid waste
Coverage: Activism, business/industry, environmental community, policy, research
Audience: Citizens, environmental organizations
Scope: National
Comment: Somewhat shrill news of community pollution and a call to arms.

Journal of Pesticide Reform
Northwest Coalition for Alternatives to Pesticides
P.O. Box 1393
Eugene, OR 97440
Phone: 503-233-5044   Fax: 503-344-0870
Mary O'Brien, Editor
Type: Journal
Frequency: Quarterly
Length: 48 pp.
Subscription fee: $25
Topics: Pest management, pesticides
Coverage: Activism, book reviews, legislation, organization activities
Audience: Citizens, environmental organizations

Scope: National
References: Yes
Comment: A fine semischolarly publication from the pesticide
    reform movement. Issues often focus on a single topic, such
    as risk assessment.

Nuclear Times

Nuclear Times, Inc.
401 Commonwealth Avenue
Boston, MA 02215
Phone: 617-266-1193 Fax: 617-266-2364
Leslie Fraser and John Tirmon, Co-Editors
Type: Newsletter
Frequency: Quarterly
Length: 60 pp.
Subscription fee: $18
Topics: Military, nuclear issues, nuclear weapons, radioactive
    waste
Coverage: Activism, organization activities
Audience: Citizens
Scope: International
Advertising: Yes
Comment: Nuclear weapons, testing, and waste are the focus
    here. This quarterly reports in particular about activist
    efforts around the world.

Pesticides and You

National Coalition Against the Misuse of Pesticides
530 Seventh Street, SE
Washington, DC 20003
Phone: 202-543-5450
Susan Cooper and Jay Feldman, Co-Editors
Type: Newsletter
Frequency: 5 issues per year
Length: 10 pp.
Subscription fee: $20
Topics: Alternative agriculture, pesticides
Coverage: Activism, legislation, litigation, organization
    activities, research

Audience: Business/industry, citizens
Scope: National
Comment: Newsbriefs mainly about new pesticide regulations and court decisions.

Toxic Times
National Toxics Campaign
37 Temple Place, 4th Floor
Boston, MA 02111
Phone: 617-482-1477   Fax: 617-232-3945
Michael Stein, Editor
Type: Newsletter
Frequency: Quarterly
Length: 24 pp.
Subscription fee: Free with membership
Topics: Hazardous substances, hazardous waste
Coverage: Activism, business/industry, environmental community, policy
Audience: Business/industry, citizens, environmental organizations
Scope: International
Comment: An activist view of the toxics threat.

❖ *Organizations*

Citizens' Clearinghouse for Hazardous Wastes
P.O. Box 926
Arlington, VA 22216
Phone: 703-237-2249
Lois Marie Gibbs, Executive Director
Purpose: Originally organized around Love Canal, this organization works on a grassroots level to inform citizens and help them protect themselves from environmental hazards. As they assess it: "The problem is so widespread that if you're not threatened now, you will be."
Founded: 1981
FYR: 1990
Revenue: [$680,000]

Expenditures: [$680,000]
1990 membership: 20,000
Staff: 13
Chapters: 60
Topics: Environmental/occupational health, hazardous sub-
stances, hazardous waste, solid waste
Approaches: Conferences, education, grassroots organizing,
policy, publications, research, technical assistance, training
Scope: National
Periodicals: *Everyone's Backyard* (newsletter)
Reports: Yes

Citizens for a Better Environment
33 E. Congress Street
Suite 523
Chicago, IL 60605
Phone: 312-939-1530
William Davis, Regional Director
Purpose: To resolve local and regional environmental prob-
lems. Current emphases are toxics use reduction and solid
waste.
Founded: 1971
FYR: 1990
Revenue: [$1,500,000]
Expenditures: [$1,500,000]
1990 membership: 30,000
Staff: 20
Chapters: 3
Topics: Hazardous substances, hazardous waste, source separa-
tion, waste reduction, water quality
Approaches: Advocacy, education, grassroots organizing, legisla-
tion, litigation, lobbying, publications
Scope: Regional (Great Lakes)
Special Projects: Toxics Use Reduction
Periodicals: *Environmental Review* (fact sheets)
Reports: Yes

Clean Sites, Inc.
1199 North Fairfax Street, Suite 400

Alexandria, VA 22314
Phone: 703-683-8522 Fax: 703-548-8773
Thomas P. Grumbly, President
Purpose: To facilitate cleanup of hazardous waste sites through federal and state programs. Clean Site professionals include mediators, project managers, attorneys, engineers, policy analysts, financial managers, chemists, computer scientists, and communications specialists.
Founded: 1984
FYR: 1990
Revenue: $5,205,557
Expenditures: $5,323,156
Staff: 50
Topics: Hazardous waste cleanup and policy, Superfund
Approaches: Conferences, policy, publications, technical assistance
Scope: National
Periodicals: *Clean Sites Forum* (newsletter)
Reports: Yes

Hazardous Materials Control Research Institute
7237 Hanover Parkway
Greenbelt, MD 20770-3602
Phone: 301-982-9500 Fax: 301-220-3870
Hal Bernard, Executive Director
Purpose: To promote better solutions for managing hazardous materials while protecting the environment
Founded: 1976
FYR: 1990
Revenues: [$2,800,000]
Expenditures: [$2,800,000]
Staff: 15
Topics: Hazardous substances
Approaches: Conferences, education, publications
Scope: National
Periodicals: *Hazardous Materials Controlled* (magazine), *FOCUS* (newsletter)
Books: Yes
Reports: Yes

National Coalition Against the Misuse of Pesticides
530 Seventh Street, SE
Washington, DC 20003
Phone: 202-543-5450
Jay Feldman, National Coordinator
Purpose: To achieve safe pesticide use and the adoption of alternative pest management strategies.
Founded: 1981
FYR: 1990
Revenue: $355,464
Expenditures: $337,417
1990 membership: 1,200
Staff: 6
Topics: Alternative pest management, hazardous substances, pesticides
Approaches: Grassroots organizing, research
Scope: National
Special projects: RCRA Reauthorization
Periodicals: *Pesticides and You* (newsletter)
Reports: Yes

National Toxics Campaign
37 Temple Place, 4th Floor
Boston, MA 02111
Phone: 617-232-0327   Fax: 617-232-3945
John O'Connor, President
Purpose: A coalition working to prevent and deal with the nation's hazardous waste problems.
Founded: 1984
FYR: 1990
Revenue: [$1,600,000]
Expenditures: [$1,600,000]
1990 membership: 150,000
Staff: 400
Affiliates: National Toxics Campaign Fund
Topics: Hazardous substances, hazardous waste, source reduction, Superfund
Approaches: Advocacy, grassroots organizing
Scope: National

Special projects: RCRA Reauthorization
Periodicals: *Toxic Times* (newsletter)
Books: Yes

Northwest Coalition for Alternatives to Pesticides
P.O. Box 1393
Eugene, OR 97440
Phone: 503-344-5044   Fax: 503-344-0870
Norma Grier, Executive Director
Purpose: To educate the public and influence public policy on
    pesticides.
Founded: 1977
FYR: 1990
Revenue: $184,701
Expenditures: $174,757
1990 membership: 1,100
Staff: 6
Topics: Agricultural chemicals, alternative pest management,
    forests, water quality
Approaches: Advocacy, conferences, direct action, education,
    grassroots organizing, legislation, policy, publications,
    training
Scope: Regional (northwestern United States)
Periodicals: *Journal of Pesticide Reform* (journal)

**Pesticide Action Network (PAN) North America Regional
    Center**
965 Mission Street, Suite 514
San Francisco, CA 94103
Phone: 415-541-9140   Fax: 415-541-9253
Monica Moore, Executive Director
Purpose: A coalition of several hundred nongovernmental
    organizations in more than fifty countries united to prevent
    pesticide proliferation and misuse.
Founded: 1982
FYR: 1990
Revenue: [$283,000]
Expenditures: [$224,000]
Staff: 7

Affiliates: 13 organizations on steering committee, 6 regional centers
Topics: Environmental health, pesticides
Approaches: Advocacy, education, lobbying
Scope: International
Periodicals: *Global Pesticide Campaign* (newsletter)
Books: Yes

Rene Dubos Center for Human Environments
100 East 8th Street
New York, NY 10028
Phone: 212-249-7745   Fax: 212-772-2033
Ruth A. Eblen, Executive Director
Purpose: To explore the interplay between man and his environment and to help develop policies for environmental conflict resolution and the creation of new environmental values.
Founded: 1972
FYR: 1990
Revenue: [$300,000]
Expenditures: [$300,000]
Staff: 8
Topics: Integrated waste management, urban issues
Approaches: Conferences, education, research
Scope: National
Special projects: The Decade of Environmental Literacy
Periodicals: *Think Globally, Act Locally* (newsletter)
Books: Yes
Reports: Yes

❑ *Foundation Funding*

In 1990, about 4 percent of the dollars awarded by U.S. independent and community foundations for environmental programs went for projects related to hazardous substances and waste.

ENVIRONMENTAL GRANT-MAKING FOUNDATIONS: FUNDING FOR TOXICS PROJECTS, 1990

Rank	Foundation	Number of Grants	Dollars Awarded
1	Great Lakes Protection Fund	10	2,014,828
2	Charles Stewart Mott Foundation	38	1,313,669
3	Public Welfare Foundation, Inc.	34	1,313,669
4	W. Alton Jones Foundation, Inc.	16	780,000
5	North Shore Unitarian Universalist Veatch Program	16	660,000
6	The Joyce Foundation	7	403,250
7	The Educational Foundation of America	8	391,000
8	The William and Flora Hewlett Foundation	5	425,000
9	The Rockefeller Foundation	3	324,500
10	Ruth Mott Fund	16	300,600

11

Endangered Lands

FROM A GLOBAL PERSPECTIVE, FOR-
ests are the most seriously endangered lands, particularly the
moist tropical forests with their abundance of species. In the
United States, all undeveloped lands are endangered from at
least from one perspective, but our ancient forests and wetlands
have aroused special concern.

ANCIENT FORESTS

Only a few hundred years ago, the United States contained some
950 million acres of primeval forest. Today, a small fraction of the
original ancient forest remains, primarily on federal lands in Oregon, Washington, Northern California, and Alaska. These
ancient forests are in a way the U.S. equivalent of the moist tropical forests. Some of them are temperate rain forests, due to their
location on the rainy west coast. They are enormously complex
ecosystems containing the tallest living things on the continent

and myriad species. The intricate food web in these forests depends on the presence of standing dead and fallen trees—a condition only found in temperate forests hundreds of years old. These forests are not only ecologically important: The ancient trees and the abundant groundcover of mosses and ferns also make them beautiful and inspiring to look at and walk through.

Eighty-five to 90 percent of the ancient forests of the Pacific Northwest (Washington, Oregon, and California) have already been cut. The old-growth timber on private land has been virtually exhausted, and logging of old-growth is now concentrated on a few million acres in the National Forests and lands administered by the Bureau of Land Management (BLM). At the current rate of cutting, all remaining ancient forests could be gone by 2023, with the exception of the 923,000 acres in wilderness areas.

The approaching demise of the ancient forests has precipitated a crisis for both the timber industry and the species that depend on these forests. In the recent past the following events have occurred:

- Logging of ancient forests increased during the 1980s, with an average of 70,000 acres being cut each year. Nevertheless, 200 sawmills closed and thousands of timber jobs were lost. Modernization of mills and export of raw logs were partly responsible.

- The Northern Spotted Owl, which requires 2000-4000 acres of old-growth forest per pair, was listed as a threatened species. The administration rejected the recommendations of a scientific panel and is crafting its own recovery plan for the owl.

- The Endangered Species Committee (known as the "God Squad") was convened to evaluate the effect of 44 planned BLM timber sales on the spotted owl. This committee has the power to exempt projects from the Endangered Species Act on economic grounds.

- The Supreme Court agreed to hear a case regarding the authority of Congress and the courts over timber sales.

Several bills have been introduced in Congress to deal with the issue of ancient forest protection and the regional economy.

The ancient forest controversy highlights the problems created when private industry becomes dependent on a publicly owned resource intended to serve multiple functions.

WETLANDS

Wetlands are dispersed throughout the United States, mostly on private land. They include coastal salt marshes, fresh-water marshes, bogs, bottomland hardwood forests, prairie potholes, playa lakes and the wet tundra of Alaska. They account for only 5 percent of the land surface in the contiguous forty-eight states, but are critical as a habitat for many species and as a moderator of the hydrologic cycle.

About one-third of U.S. endangered and threatened species depend on wetland habitats. Between 60 and 90 percent of our commercial fish spawn or develop in coastal wetlands.

Wetlands are essential to the hydrologic cycle. They help control floods, reduce erosion, recharge groundwater, and improve water quality. Yet less than half the original 215 million wetlands acres in the contiguous forty-eight states remain. Between 300,000 and 500,000 acres are being destroyed each year. This has had a devastating effect on breeding populations of certain waterfowl.

The federal government regulates wetland development under the Clean Water Act, the Farm Bill and other laws. In order to consolidate the definition of wetlands used by various federal agencies, the Army Corps of Engineers, EPA, Soil Conservation Service and Fish and Wildlife Service produced a federal wetlands delineation manual in 1989. It gave wetlands a new definition, which increased the amount of acreage under federal protection, and led to a backlash by industry, developers, and farmers. Several bills now pending in Congress would redefine federal jurisdiction over wetlands, in some cases removing protections in effect since the 1970s and requiring compensation to landowners for restricting development.

Early in his administration, President Bush promised a policy of "no net loss of wetlands." But the White House Council on

Competitiveness has recently proposed a revision in the federal manual that would remove up to 50 percent of the nation's wetlands from protection.

The concept of *no net loss* includes the increasingly popular practice of creating new wetlands to replace those destroyed. This practice has had mixed success; it is not easy to create a functioning hydrological and biological system from scratch.

The wetlands dispute highlights the problem of how to deal with privately-owned lands that are thought to provide greater benefits to society as a whole than to their owners.

LAND PROTECTION

The acquisition and management of protected lands is a subject of perennial interest, with a diverse literature and a variety of opportunities for citizen participation. Public lands are not synonymous with protected lands. In the United States, for example, of the 26 percent of land under federal jurisdiction, only 4 percent is wilderness; the remainder is open to various consumptive uses. The following outline describes some of the more important types of lands under federal protection.

NATIONAL PARKS

The National Park Service oversees 357 units and a total of 80 million acres. The first national park was Yellowstone, created in 1872. In more recent years, national parks have been established near urban areas. The national parks are under considerable stress; a 1980 Park Service report identified 73 different threats to the parks, and many of the problems have worsened since then. Some of the issues facing the parks:

1. *Population pressures.* Recreational visits numbered 233.4 million in 1985 and are expected to reach 346.7 million by 2000. The ranger staff and maintenance budgets are insufficient to handle this use. In popular areas, problems include traffic jams and public demand for more shops, hotels, and roads. In less accessible areas, the parks are plagued by illegal activities such as vandalism and poaching.

2. *Boundary problems.* Development (such as logging, mining and resort construction) near national park borders jeopardizes the integrity of migratory species as well as resident park flora and fauna. The Yellowstone ecosystem, for instance, extends far beyond the borders of the park. Bear, moose, and other species need the greater scope of rangelands to carry out their natural migratory patterns.

3. *Air pollution.* from cities and power plants obscures views in the Grand Canyon and other parks.

NATIONAL FORESTS

The largest agency in the Department of Agriculture, the Forest Service manages 191 million acres in 156 national forests, 71 experimental forests, and 19 national grasslands. From their inception in 1891, the national forests have provided timber, water, grazing, and minerals. Timber is sold to private companies on a bid basis. In addition, the national forests receive more recreational visitors than any other public land area. Some of the issues facing the national forests:

1. *Conflicting mandates.* Laws passed in the 1960s and 1970s require the Forest Service to protect fish and wildlife, watersheds, biodiversity, and ecological systems, and to maintain viable populations of existing vertebrate species. But members of Congress from timber-producing areas are still able to mandate timber harvest goals that undermine these other priorities.

   For example, in Alaska's Tongass National Forest, until the end of 1990 the Forest Service was committed to harvest 4.5 billion board feet over 10 years. This commitment was supported by a $40 million per year congressional appropriation to ensure the harvest and timber supply for the local "dependent industry." Thus, in effect, the U.S. taxpayer has been paying the Forest Service up to $40 million per year to destroy a rare and irreplaceable temperate rain forest for the benefit of two large lumber companies, one foreign-owned. In November 1990, after a monumental effort spearheaded by the Wilderness Society, Congress passed the Tongass Timber Reform Act. The Act sets aside 6 million acres as wilderness, eliminating these acres from the area subject to Forest Service logging and the automatic subsidies for that logging. But 10 million acres remain within the Tongass, still available for logging. And now the Forest Service has recommended in its revised Tongass Land Management Plan that the annual timber cut be raised to 450 million board feet, compared to the annual average of 298 million board feet cut during the 1980s.

The problem persists in other national forests as well. In 1991, a forester in charge of the Northern Rockies region was pressured to resign when he refused to meet logging targets on the grounds that they were incompatible with resource protection laws.

2. *Below-cost Timber Sales.* About 10 billion to 11 billion board feet of wood is logged in the national forests each year. Although private companies do the logging, the Forest Service builds the access roads and administers the sales. Overall, receipts fall far short of costs. Cutting the national forests costs taxpayers from $250 to $500 million each year.

BUREAU OF LAND MANAGEMENT LANDS

The Bureau of Land Management (BLM) was formed in 1946 from the old General Land Office and the Grazing Service. Most of its land is in the west, where the public domain was never completely sold or granted to homesteaders. The BLM manages 270 million acres including deserts, grasslands and forests. Some of the areas are as spectacular as the national parks but much less widely known. Some of the issues facing the BLM lands:

1. *Conflicting Uses.* BLM lands are the subject of controversy among different user groups, such as off-road vehicle (ORV) users and wilderness advocates. They also tend to suffer from the illegal uses common to many backcountry areas.

2. *Overgrazing.* Private ranchers have grazed cattle on BLM land since the last century. Grazing fees on federal land are much lower than those on private land—sometimes only one-tenth as much. In addition, overgrazing has significantly damaged native range grasses and riparian habitats. Some people feel the taxpayers are subsidizing overgrazing of our public lands; others are concerned that raising the grazing fees would bankrupt ranchers.

NATIONAL WILDLIFE REFUGES

The National Wildlife Refuge System was established in 1903 to protect important wildlife areas such as wetlands used by migratory birds. The refuge system contains 90 million acres in over 450 units, and is open to visitors. At first, hunting and trapping were not allowed in the refuges, but since the late 1940s these uses have been expanding. They are now permitted in more than half the areas. Some of the issues facing wildife refuges:

1. *Demand for Nonwildlife Uses.* A 1988 report by the Government Accounting Office stated that the demand for nonwildlife uses was "increasingly diverting refuge management attention and scarce resources away from wildlife management." Other uses include grazing, ORV use, powerboating and military bombing maneuvers.

2. *Pollution.* The wildlife refuges also suffer the effects of pollution from surrounding land uses. For example, at the Kesterton Wildlife Refuge in California waterfowl are being poisoned by contaminated agricultural drainage.

The greatest controversy at present surrounds the decision on whether to drill for oil in the Arctic National Wildlife Refuge on the north coast of Alaska.

WILDERNESS AREAS

The Wilderness Act of 1964 established the process of creating wilderness areas out of roadless lands on federal property. Each new wilderness area must be established by an act of Congress, and the system is being continually expanded. There are now 94.9 million acres of wilderness, which are included within national parks, forests, and BLM lands. Wilderness areas allow for the undisturbed functioning of natural ecosystems, at least within their limited areas. They are used by hikers and backpackers and in some cases for grazing, mining, and hunting. But they may not be used for logging or construction projects such as dams and roads.

OTHER FEDERAL LANDS

Other federal lands include the National Lakeshores, National Monuments, National Recreation Areas, National Seashores, National Trails, and Wild and Scenic Rivers.

STATE, LOCAL, AND PRIVATE CONSERVATION

Unlike federal lands, which are concentrated in the west, state and local parks can be found throughout the United States. The state parks contain over 10 million acres. Trails, greenways, and local parks are also significant in protecting natural habitat and human quality of life. Where government has been unable to protect important lands, private land trusts and conservation organizations often step in to negotiate sales, easements, or bequests with landowners. The Nature Conservancy is the best known of these organizations, but small local land trusts are proliferating throughout the country.

UNITED NATIONS BIOSPHERE RESERVES

The United Nations Educational, Scientific and Cultural Organization (UNESCO) since 1971 has designated world biosphere reserves in order to protect natural landscapes and traditional human land use patterns. Each reserve has a relatively undisturbed natural core area, a buffer zone where compatible human activities can go on, and a transition zone. There are biosphere reserves in over 70 countries throughout the world. Those in the United States are essentially honorary designations of existing protected areas.

RESOURCES

☙ Books and Reports

Alternatives to Deforestation: Steps Toward Sustainable Use of the Amazon Rain Forest. Anthony B. Anderson, editor. New York: Columbia University Press. 1990, 281 pp.

Conserving Biological Diversity in Our National Forests. The Ecological Society of America. Washington, DC: The Wilderness Society. 1986, 115 pp.

Cutting Our Losses: Policy Reform to Sustain Tropical Forest Resources. Chip Barber. Washington, DC: World Resources Institute. 1991, 88 pp.

The Dilemma of Wilderness. Corry McDonald. Santa Fe, NM: Sunstone Press. 1987, 115 pp.

The Economics of Afforestation: A Case Study in Africa. Dennis Anderson. Occasional Paper Number 1/New Series. Washington, DC: The World Bank. 1987, 86 pp.

The Fate of the Forest: Developers, Destroyers and Defenders of the Amazon. Susanna Hecht and Alexander Cockburn. New York: HarperCollins Publishers. 1990, 357 pp.

The Forest and the Trees: A Guide to Excellent Forestry. Gordon Robinson. Washington, DC: Island Press. 1988, 257 pp.

Lessons of the Rainforest. Suzanne Head and Robert Heinzman, editors. San Francisco: Sierra Club Books. 1990, 275 pp.

The Man Who Planted Trees. Jean Giono. Chelsea, VT: Chelsea Green Publishing Company. 1985, 52 pp.

The Monkey Wrench Gang. Edward Abbey. New York: Avon Books. 1975, 387 pp.

The Nation's Forest Resources. Roger A. Sedjo. Washington, DC: Resources for the Future. 1990, 85 pp.

Old Growth in the Pacific Northwest: A Status Report. P. H. Morrison. Washington, DC: The Wilderness Society. 1988, 53 pp.

Playing God in Yellowstone: The Destruction of America's First National Park. Alston Chase. New York: Harcourt Brace Jovanovich, Publishers. 1987, 464 pp.

Public Policies and the Misuse of Forests. Robert Repetto and Malcolm Gillis, editors. World Resources Institute. New York: Cambridge University Press. 1988, 432 pp.

Recent International Developments Impacting United States Forest Products Trade. A. Clark Wiseman. Washington, DC: Resources for the Future. 1990, 55 pp.

Reforming the Forest Service. Randal O'Toole. Washington, DC: Island Press. 1988, 247 pp.

Saving the Tropical Forests. Judith Gradwohl and Russell Greenbert, Smithsonian Institution. Washington, DC: Island Press. 1988, 214 pp.

Trees: A Celebration. Jill Fairchild, editor. New York: Weidenfeld & Nicholson. 1989, 111 pp.

Trees of Life: Protecting Tropical Forests and Their Biological Wealth. Kenton Miller and Laura Tangley. Washington, DC: World Resources Institute. 1991, 224 pp.

Wildlands: Their Protection and Management in Economic Development. George Ledec and Robert Goodland. Washington, DC: The World Bank. 1988, 278 pp.

✪ Periodicals

American Forests
American Forestry Association
1516 P Street, NW
Washington, DC 20005
Phone: 202-667-3300   Fax: 202-667-7751
Bill Rooney, Editor
Type: Magazine
Frequency: Bimonthly
Length: 82 pp.

Subscription fee: $24
Topics: Endangered species, forestry, forests, pest management, public lands, recreation, wildlife
Coverage: Organization activities, policy, research
Audience: Citizens
Scope: National
Advertising: Yes
Comment: A good way to distinguish the forest from the trees with a wide range of articles on logging, private woodlots, urban forests, disease control, and wildlife.

Arid Lands Newsletter
University of Arizona, Office of Arid Lands Studies
Geology Building
Tucson, AZ 85719
Phone: 602-621-1955   Fax: 602-621-3816
Emily E. Whitehead, Editor
Type: Newsletter
Frequency: Semiannual
Length: 20 pp.
Subscription fee: Free
Topics: Drylands, soils
Coverage: Research
Audience: Professional/academic
Scope: International
References: Yes
Comment: Short, elegant pieces on desert flora, fauna, and habitat.

Earth First! The Radical Environmental Journal
Earth First! Journal, Inc.
P.O. Box 5871
Tucson, AZ 85703
John Davis, Editor
Type: Newsletter
Frequency: 8 issues per year
Length: 40 pp.
Subscription fee: $20
Topics: Forests, rivers/streams, wildlife

Coverage: Activism, environmental community, policy
Audience: Citizens, environmental organizations
Scope: Mixed
References: Yes
Advertising: Yes
Comment: Lively and not without appeal like the parent organi-
zation, perhaps because EarthFirst!ers seem to act on their
convictions, albeit not always with a subtle touch. Currently
in the process of regrouping and may be hard to reach.

Forest and Conservation History
Forest History Society
701 Vickers Avenue
Durham, NC 27701
Phone: 919-682-9319
David O. Percy, Editor
Type: Journal
Frequency: Quarterly
Length: 40 pp.
Subscription fee: $25
Topics: Conservation, forests, wilderness, wildlife
Coverage: Book reviews, research
Audience: Citizens, professional/academic
Scope: International
References: Yes
Comment: Articles describing the evolution of conservation pol-
itics and the perceptions of nature as well as the history of
forest products and industries.

Journal of Forestry
Executive Enterprises, Inc.
22 West 21st Street
New York, NY 10010-6904
Phone: 212-645-7880   Fax: 212-675-4883
N. Taylor Gregg, Editor
Type: Journal
Frequency: Monthly
Length: 50 pp.
Subscription fee: $45

Topics: Forestry, wilderness
Coverage: Book reviews, business/industry, environmental community, organization activities, research
Audience: Professional/academic
Scope: International
References: Yes
Advertising: Yes
Comment: About forestry science, technology, practices, and education. Articles frequently deal with conservation issues.

National Parks

National Parks and Conservation Association
1015 31st Street, NW, 4th Floor
Washington, DC 20007
Phone: 202-944-8530   Fax: 202-944-8535
Michele Strutin, Editor
Type: Magazine
Frequency: Bimonthly
Length: 50 pp.
Subscription fee: $2.50
Topics: Ecology, ecosystems, forests, national parks, recreation, wildlife
Coverage: Organization activities, policy, research
Audience: Citizens
Scope: National
Advertising: Yes
Comment: What's happening in our national parks, including ecological events (such as decline of amphibian populations), controversies (to burn or not to burn), and descriptions of noteworthy places.

Natural Areas Journal

Natural Areas Association
320 South Third Street
Rockford, IL 61104
Phone: 815-964-6666
Greg F. Iffrig, Editor
Type: Journal
Frequency: Quarterly

Length: 100 pp.
Subscription fee: $25
Topics: Ecosystem restoration
Coverage: Business/industry, environmental community, research
Audience: Professional/academic
Scope: Regional (Midwest)
References: Yes
Comment: Data on current projects in restoration ecology: Who's doing what and where to go for more information.

The Nature Conservancy Magazine
The Nature Conservancy, Headquarters
1815 North Lynn Street
Arlington, VA 22209
Phone: 703-841-5300   Fax: 703-841-1283
Sue Dodge, Editor
Type: Magazine
Frequency: Bimonthly
Length: 40 pp.
Subscription fee: $25
Topics: Biosphere reserves, ecosystem restoration, land acquisition
Coverage: Activism, policy, research
Audience: Citizens, environmental organizations
Scope: International
Comment: Eloquently documents The Nature Conservancy's efforts to research, protect, and restore biodiversity worldwide by acquiring and protecting endangered lands.

Northwest Renewable Resources Center Newsletter
Northwest Renewable Resources Center
710 2nd Avenue, Suite 1133
Seattle, WA 98104
Phone: 206-623-7361   Fax: 206-467-1640
Amy Solomon, Director
Type: Newsletter
Frequency: Quarterly
Length: 4 pp.

Subscription fee: Free

Topics: Conflict resolution, fisheries, forests, land use, Native Americans, renewable resources, water use, wildlife

Coverage: Organization activities, policy

Audience: Citizens

Scope: Regional

Comment: About mediation and other efforts to preserve the environmental resources of the Northwestern states.

Restoration and Management Notes

University of Wisconsin Press

144 North Murray Street

Madison, WI 53715

Phone: 608-262-4952   Fax: 608-262-7560

William R. Jordan III, Editor

Type: Newsletter

Frequency: Semiannual

Length: 50 pp.

Subscription fee: $15

Topics: Biodiversity, ecosystems, ecosystem restoration, endangered species, riparian lands, rivers/streams

Coverage: Environmental community, research

Audience: Citizens, professional/academic

Scope: National

References: Yes

Advertising: Yes

Comment: It is no longer enough to conserve: We must repair the damage we've done to the Earth. This publication describes the new activist wave in ecology.

Urban Forests

American Forestry Association

1516 P Street, NW

Washington, DC 20005

Phone: 202-667-3300   Fax: 202-667-7751

Gary Moll, Editor

Type: Magazine

Frequency: Bimonthly

Length: 24 pp.

Subscription fee: Free
Topics: Urban forests
Coverage: Activism, business/industry, policy, research
Audience: Citizens, environmental organizations, professionals
Scope: International
Comment: Practical articles promoting forestry and conservation in urban areas, where trees now have some cachet, thanks to global warming.

Wilderness

Wilderness Society
1400 Eye Street, NW
Washington, DC 20005
Phone: 202-833-2300   Fax: 202-429-3958
T. H. Watkins, Editor
Type: Magazine
Frequency: Quarterly
Length: 70 pp.
Subscription fee: Free with membership
Topics: Conservation, ecological ethics, forests, protected lands, wilderness, wildlife
Coverage: Book reviews, policy, research
Audience: Citizens
Scope: National
Advertising: Yes
Comment: Both a celebration of wild, beautiful areas and a discussion of the factors that threaten them.

❖ Organizations

American Forest Service Employees for Environmental Ethics
Box 1165
Eugene, OR 97440
Phone: 503-484-2692   Fax: 503-484-3004
Jeff DeBonis, Executive Director
Founded: 1989
Purpose: Even Forest Service employees cannot live with the destructive policies of the Service. Founded by Mr. DeBonis,

AFSEEE advocates a socially responsible value system for The Service, based on a land ethic ensuring ecologically and economically sustainable management.

FYR: 1990

Revenue: $148,530

Expenditures: $120,275

1990 membership: 5,200

Change from 1989: +44%

Staff: 5

Chapters: 10

Topics: Ancient forests, conservation, environmental ethics, forests, forest management, stewardship, U.S. Forest Service, wilderness

Approaches: Advocacy, direct action, education, grassroots organizing, lobbying, policy, publications

Special projects: To end hard targets, to promote free speech by government employees, protection of ancient forests and roadless areas

Periodicals: *Inner Voice* (newsletter)

American Forestry Association

1516 P Street, NW

P.O. Box 2000

Washington, DC 20013-2000

Phone: 202-667-3300   Fax: 202-667-7751

Charles Tarver, President

Purpose: To increase citizens' awareness, concern, and active involvement in both private and public actions and policies affecting U.S. forests.

Founded: 1875

FYR: 1990

Revenue: [$3,300,000]

Expenditures: [$3,300,000]

1990 membership: 125,000

Change from 1989: +35%

Staff: 25

Topics: Forests

Approaches: Advocacy, education, policy, publications, research

Scope: National

Special projects: The Global ReLeaf Campaign
Periodicals: *American Forests* (magazine), *Urban Forests* (magazine), *Resource Hotline* (newsletter), *The Global ReLeaf Report* (newsletter)
Reports: Yes

Earth First!
P.O. Box 5871
Tucson, AZ 85703
Dave Foreman, Founder
Purpose: Currently in disarray (and without a current phone number), this organization was founded to preserve the natural environment using a no-compromise approach. Earth First! espouses what it calls nonviolent ecodefense. It has been important in bringing environmental issues before the public.
FYR: 1988
Revenue: $109,000
Expenditures: $55,000
Topics: Forests, marine mammals, wilderness, wildlife
Approaches: Advocacy, direct action, grassroots organizing, publications
Scope: International
Special projects: Ancient Forests, Amazonian Artists
Periodicals: *Earth First* (newsletter)
Books: Yes
Reports: Yes

National Parks and Conservation Association
1015 31st Street, NW, 4th Floor
Washington, DC 20007
Phone: 202-944-8530   Fax: 202-944-8535
Paul C. Pritchard, President
Purpose: Through Congress NPCA works as a watchdog organization to encourage legislation to benefit the parks, besieged as they are by problems of overuse, pollution, and encroaching development.
Founded: 1919

FYR: 1990
Revenue: $6,046,629
Expenditures: $6,046,629
1990 membership: 270,000
Change from 1989: +40%
Staff: 40
Chapters: 5
Affiliates: New York State Parks and Conservation Association
Topics: Acid rain, air pollution, conservation, habitats, national parks, off-road vehicles, real estate development, recreation
Approaches: Advocacy, conferences, education, grassroots organizing, lobbying, policy, publications, research
Scope: National
Periodicals: *National Parks* (magazine)
Reports: Yes

Native Forest Council
P.O. Box 2171
Eugene, OR 97402
Phone: 503-461-2156   Fax: 503-461-2156
Timothy Hermach, Executive Director
Purpose: To protect public forest lands throughout the United States.
Founded: 1988
FYR: 1990
Revenue: [$200,000]
Expenditures: [$200,000]
1990 membership: 15,000
Change from 1989: +15%
Staff: 6
Affiliates: Native Forest Action Council
Topics: Ancient forests, native forests
Approaches: Direct action, education, grassroots organizing, publications, research
Scope: National
Special projects: National Media Campaign
Periodicals: *The Forest Voice* (newsletter)

Natural Areas Association

320 South Third Street
Rockford, IL 61104
Phone: 815-964-6666   Fax: 217-244-5792
David N. Paddock, Executive Director
Purpose: To advance the preservation of natural diversity by informing, uniting and supporting people who identify, protect, manage, and study natural areas and biological diversity.
Founded: 1979
FYR: 1990
Revenue: $91,000
Expenditures: $83,000
1990 membership: 2,100
Change from 1989: +15%
Staff: 4
Topics: Biodiversity, land conservation
Approaches: Conferences, education, publications
Scope: International
Periodicals: *Natural Areas Journal* (journal)

Northwest Renewable Resources Center

1133 Dexter Horton Building
710 Second Avenue
Seattle, WA 98104
Phone: 206-623-7361   Fax: 206-467-1640
Amy Solomon, Executive Director
Purpose: Founded by leaders of industry, Native American tribes, and environmental organizations to create a structure for conflict resolution of natural resource issues.
Founded: 1984
FYR: 1990
Revenue: [$395,000]
Expenditures: [$340,000]
Staff: 6
Topics: Fish, forests, Native Americans, natural resource protection, water allocation, wildlife
Approaches: Dispute resolution, policy, training
Scope: Regional

Special projects: Timber/Fish/Wildlife Project, Indian Land
    Tenure and Economic Development, Joint Management
    Project, State of Alaska Forest Practices Act Review, Idaho
    Water Antidegradation Policy Agreement
Periodicals: *Northwest Renewable Resources Center* (newsletter)
Reports: Yes

Rainforest Action Network
301 Broadway, Suite A
San Francisco, CA 94133
Phone: 415-398-4404   Fax: 415-398-2732
Randall Hayes, Director
Purpose: To stop the destruction of tropical rain forests around
    the world.
Founded: 1985
FYR: 1990
Revenue: [$1,200,000]
Expenditures: [$1,150,000]
1990 membership: 35,000
Staff: 10 to 15
Chapters: 120 action groups
Topics: Conservation, rain forests
Approaches: Advocacy, conferences, direct action, dispute reso-
    lution, education, funding, grassroots organizing, publica-
    tions, research
Scope: Global
Special projects: Tropical Timber Campaign, Amazonian Cam-
    paign, Hawaii Campaign
Periodicals: *World Rainforest Report* (newsletter), *Action Alert*
    (newsletter)
Books: Yes
Reports: Yes

Society for Range Management
1839 York Street
Denver, CO 80206
Phone: 303-355-7070   Fax: 303-355-5059
Peter V. Jackson, Executive Vice-President

Purpose: To promote the development, study, effective management, wise use, and understanding of the world's rangelands.
Founded: 1948
FYR: 1990
Revenue: $517,000
Expenditures: $499,000
1990 membership: 5,300
Change from 1989: +13%
Staff: 8
Chapters: 20
Affiliates: Yes
Topics: Land use, natural resource management, rangelands
Approaches: Direct action, publications, research
Scope: International
Periodicals: *Journal of Range Management* (journal), *Rangelands* (magazine)
Books: Yes
Reports: Yes

Society of American Foresters

5400 Grosvenor Lane
Bethesda, MD 20814
Phone: 301-897-8720   Fax: 301-897-3690
William F. Banzhaf, Executive Vice-President
Purpose: To advance the science, technology, education, and practice of professional forestry for the benefit of human society.
Founded: 1900
FYR: 1990
Revenue: $2,600,000
Expenditures: $2,800,000
1990 membership: 20,000
Staff: 30
Chapters: 244
Topics: Acid rain, forestry, global warming, national forests, national parks
Approaches: Conferences, education, publications
Scope: National

Periodicals: *Journal of Forestry* (journal), *Forest Science* (journal)
Reports: Yes

Trust for Public Land
116 New Montgomery Street
San Francisco, CA 94105
Phone: 415-495-4014   Fax: 415-495-4103
Martin J. Rosen, President
Purpose: Working with community groups, public agencies, and other nonprofit organizations to protect endangered lands through acquisitions.
Founded: 1972
FYR: 1990
Revenue: $21,000,000
Expenditures: $18,800,000
Staff: 185
Chapters: 12
Topics: Conservation, natural resources
Approaches: Conferences, education, land acquisition
Scope: National
Special projects: National Land Counselor Program
Periodicals: *Land and People* (magazine), *Open Views* (newsletter)

Wilderness Society
900 Seventeenth Street, NW
Washington, DC 20006
Phone: 202-833-2300   Fax: 202-429-3945
George T. Frampton, Jr., President
Purpose: To promote the protection and wise management of federal public lands.
Founded: 1935
FYR: 1990
Revenue: $17,900,000
Expenditures: $17,700,000
1990 membership: 400,000
Staff: 130
Chapters: 15
Topics: Ecosystems, forests, public lands, wilderness

Approaches: Advocacy, education, legislation, lobbying, publications, research
Scope: National
Special projects: Ancient Forests of the Pacific Northwest, Arctic National Wildlife Refuge, Endangered Species
Periodicals: *Wilderness* (magazine)
Books: Yes
Reports: Yes

❏ Foundation Funding

In 1990, of the dollars awarded for environmental programs by U.S. independent and community foundations, about 27 percent went for the protection of endangered lands.

❏   ENVIRONMENTAL GRANT-MAKING FOUNDATIONS: ❏
FUNDING FOR ENDANGERED LANDS, 1990

Rank	Foundation	Number of Grants	Dollars Awarded
1	Richard King Mellon Foundation	7	22,423,476
2	John D. and Catherine T. MacArthur Foundation	33	8,893,062
3	National Fish and Wildlife Foundation	28	4,446,950
4	The Ford Foundation	26	3,497,000
5	W. K. Kellogg Foundation	2	2,026,334
6	The Champlin Foundations	1	2,000,000
7	The J. M. Kaplan Fund, Inc.	42	1,885,500
8	W. Alton Jones Foundation, Inc.	26	1,796,850
9	The Andrew W. Mellon Foundation	4	1,527,900
10	American Conservation Association, Inc.	35	1,410,000

12

Development

Sustainable development. Ungainly as the term sounds, it's the latest buzzword at the U.S. Agency for International Development. At The World Bank officials swear by it. Third World economists say it is the answer to their future. Plainly, it's an idea whose time has come.

NORMAN MYERS, 1989

SUSTAINABLE DEVELOPMENT HAS achieved buzzword status in just the few years since the publication of *Our Common Future,* the 1987 report by the World Commission on Environment and Development. In its simplest form, sustainable development means that economic growth and the conservation of natural resources not only can but *must* coexist. According to Gro Harlem Brundtland, Prime Minister of Norway and head of the Commission:

> The "environment" is where we all live; and "development" is what we all do in attempting to improve our lot within that abode.
> The two are inseparable.

The concept of sustainable development grew from a realistic—and somewhat grim—assessment of the state of the world in the late 1980s. In summary:

1. The human population has doubled twice since 1900 and is now over 5 billion. It is expected to double again before stabilizing somewhere around 10 billion in the next century. Ninety percent of the growth will occur in the less developed countries (LDCs) where nearly 40 percent of the population is under age sixteen.

2. The developed world, which consumes most of the Earth's resources, has expanded enormously during the twentieth century:

    *   *Economic activity* has grown twentyfold since 1900. It may increase another five to ten times in the next fifty years.

    *   *Industrial activity* has grown fiftyfold in the last century, 80 percent of this since 1950. Much of this growth has come from the use of forests, soils, seas, and waterways.

    *   *Fossil fuel consumption* has increased thirtyfold since 1900.

3. The gap between rich and poor nations is increasing: most LDCs now have lower per capita incomes than in 1980. There are more hungry and illiterate people in the world than ever before.

4. Environmental degradation is occurring worldwide. Drastic changes in climate and atmosphere are occurring because of human activities:

    *   Each year 2.4 million acres of productive soil turn into desert.

    *   Each year 4.5 million acres of forest are cut down.

    *   Fresh water is becoming increasingly scarce.

Until recently, policymakers focused on how economic growth adversely affects the environment. We are now beginning to realize that the various forms of ecological stress—degradation of soils, waters, atmosphere, and forests—also jeopardize our economic future. We are, in a way, all "downwind, downstream."

The solution to the rapid deterioration of our habitat lies in recognition that there must be limits to human population growth and use of natural resources:

1. Population growth must be controlled.

2. Energy must be conserved and new, less environmentally destructive forms of energy developed. Present modes of agriculture must be altered. Water-use practices must change. Species variation must be preserved. Commons of the planet, such as the oceans, atmosphere and space, and Antarctica, must be conserved so as to avoid what Garrett Hardin called "The Tragedy of the Commons."

3. The gap between the "North," the 33 more developed or industrialized countries (MDCs), and the "South," the remaining 142 LDCs, must be narrowed.

    *   LDCs contain 4 billion people, or 77 percent of the world's population, but use only about 20 percent of the world's energy and mineral resources. Nearly a billion of those people live in utter poverty. They cannot be ignored, because their actions now affect us all. The landless cut down trees, endangering lands and their resident species, as well as the global climate and atmosphere.

    *   For the most part, the LDCs have resource-based economies. Their long-term economic development depends on maintaining, if not increasing, their natural resource stocks. But in the last twenty years, forests, grasslands, soils, waters, and other natural commodities have instead been depleted.

    *   International debt, now greater than $1.3 trillion with more than $60 billion a year in interest pay-

ments, is the central problem. The developing world now pays more to the developed world than it receives. It also "pays" more than its share of the environmental costs of global GNP, since degradation of its lands and waters tends to be most severe.

- Farmers in North America, Western Europe, and Japan receive subsidies worth more than $300 billion a year that encourage them to farm marginal lands, clear forests, overuse chemicals, and waste water. Their produce is then dumped on the world market, undercutting commodities from the LDCs.

- To pay off their debt, the LDCs have been encouraged to increase exports by developing cash crops. In the process, they have lost the ability to feed their own populations. Their commodities now don't pay enough; to increase income, they cultivate more marginal land. The result has been a loss of natural resources and loss of economic sustainability.

Sustainable development is thus a fashionable concept. But it has at least two enormous failings:

- It does not explain how the economy of the MDCs can expand when there is less and less space in the world for the products and waste humans produce.

- It also assumes that LDCs want to "progress," yet will be content with a different sort of progress than the MDCs have experienced.

Nonetheless, because sustainable development in some form is probably our only option, efforts to foster it are under way on many fronts. Some examples include:

- Ecological economics which seeks to integrate environmental concerns with economics in developing policy. In particular, this discipline recomputes costs so that environmental costs are internalized.

- Financial support for developing countries. The World-watch Institute has estimated that a total investment of $149 billion is needed by the year 2000 to slow population growth, protect soils, reforest degraded lands, raise energy efficiency, develop renewable energy, and retire debt. In *Natural Endowments: Financing Resource Conservation for Development,* World Resources Institute estimates a need for $20 billion to $50 billion per year and outlines four possible mechanisms to deliver this support:

  (1) An international environmental facility to help coordinate the work of existing agencies and lending institutions on conservation projects.

  (2) Investments for sustainable resource use by the private sector through a pilot "Ecovest" program.

  (3) Innovative approaches to debt reduction including larger debt-for-nature schemes and bilateral debt-conversion programs.

  (4) A global environmental trust fund designed to slow down the accumulation of greenhouse gases and help maintain ecosystems in the developing world.

One of the mechanisms most discussed to date is the debt-for-nature swap, developed as it became clear that much of the international Third World debt could never be fully repaid. The first swap was made in July 1987, when Conservation International used a $100,000 grant from the Weeden Foundation to buy $650,000 worth of Bolivia's $4 billion debt. In exchange for debt cancellation, Bolivia agreed to establish three protected areas around the Beni Biosphere Reserve in the Andean foothills. Other debt-for-nature swaps have taken place in several other Latin American countries, including Ecuador and Costa Rica, and in the Philippines.

Debt-for-nature swaps are now not considered the ultimate solution, because the secondary market for devalued debt is less than 1 percent of the Third World's external debt. Further, such projects do not guarantee the success of a conservation area—hence the other schemes to reform international lending patterns. The fact that The World Bank has instituted a new global environment program is a hopeful sign that reform may be under way.

- Finally, smaller scale efforts in sustainability are occurring in MDCs and LDCs all over the world. One example is occurring in western Amazonia, where a team from the New York Botanical Garden has devised a way to use the produce of the rain forest without cutting it down. One acre of forest fruits and rubber generates six times the income derived from logging—and it will continue forever.

RESOURCES

✍ Books and Reports

Economic Policies for Maximizing Nature Tourism's Contribution to Sustainable Development. Kerg Lindberg. Washington, DC: World Resources Institute. 1991, 30 pp.

Natural Endowments: Financing Resource Conservation for Development. Washington, DC: World Resources Institute. 1989, 33 pp.

Promoting Environmentally Sound Economic Progress: What the North Can Do. Robert Repetto. Washington, DC: World Resources Institute. 1990, 20 pp.

A Review of the World Bank Forestry Sector Project to the Republic of Cote D'Ivoire. David Reed and Jennifer Smith. Washington, DC: World Wildlife Fund. 1990, 21 pp.

Sustainable Development: Exploring the Contradictions. Michael Redclift. London: Methuen & Company, Ltd. 1987, 221 pp.

Sustainable Development of the Biosphere. William C. Clark and R. E. Munn, editors. New York: Cambridge University Press. 1986, 491 pp.

Sustaining Tomorrow: A Strategy for World Conservation and Development. Francis R. Thibodeau and Hermann H. Field, editors. Hanover, NH: University Press of New England. 1984, 186 pp.

Transforming Technology: An Agenda for Environmentally Sustainable Growth in the Twenty-first Century. George Heath, Robert Repetto, and Rodney Sobin. Washington, DC: World Resources Institute. 1991, 40 pp.

Wasting Assets: Natural Resources in the National Income Accounts. Robert Repetto, William Magrath, Michael Wells, Christine Beer, and Fabrizio Rossini. Washington, DC: World Resource Institute. 1989, 68 pp.

World Development Report 1991. The World Bank. New York: Oxford University Press. 1991, 304 pp.

✪ Periodicals

In Context
Context Institute
P.O. Box 11470
Bainbridge Island, WA 98110
Phone: 206-842-0216   Fax: 206-842-5208
Robert Gilman, Editor
Type: Magazine
Frequency: Quarterly
Length: 65 pp.
Subscription fee: $18
Topics: Environmental ethics, sustainability
Scope: International
Audience: Citizens
Comment: Short engaging pieces that explore individual and group efforts to develop a humane sustainable culture around the world.

❖ Organizations

Bank Information Center
2000 P Street, Suite 515
Washington, DC 20036
Phone: 202-822-6630   Fax: 202-822-6644
Chad Dobson, Secretary
Purpose: To act as a clearinghouse for environmental informa-
    tion on development projects funded by The World Bank
    and the International Monetary Fund. (The World Bank
    alone had a loan portfolio of about $32 billion in 1990.)
    Using this information, nongovernmental organizations
    (NGOs) of the North and the South can better integrate
    their efforts to influence the policies of the multilateral
    development banks.
Founded: 1985
FYR: 1988 and 1989
Revenue: $182,545
Expenditures: $197,209
Staff: 3
Topics: Developing countries, development, multilateral devel-
    opment banks, NGOs
Approaches: Conferences, funding, information services, publi-
    cations, research, technical assistance
Scope: International
Special projects: New Forest Project, United Nations Confer-
    ence on Economic Development (UNCED) 1992
Reports: Yes

Conservation International
1015 18th Street, NW
Washington, DC 20036
Phone: 202-429-5660   Fax: 202-887-5188
Russell A. Mittermeier, President
Purpose: To conserve ecosystems and biological diversity by
    building indigenous local support in more than twenty coun-
    tries in the Neotropics, Africa, Asia, and North America.
Founded: 1987
FYR: 1990

Revenue: $8,288,216
Expenditures: $8,221,493
1990 membership: 55,000
Staff: 70
Affiliates: Ecotrust
Topics: Biodiversity, biosphere reserves, inventories, sustainable development, tropical rain forests
Approaches: Debt-for-nature exchanges, direct action, education, policy, research, technical assistance
Scope: International
Periodicals: *Tropicus* (newsletter)

Cultural Survival
11 Divinity Avenue
Cambridge, MA 02138
Phone: 617-495-2562   Fax: 617-495-1396
Pam Solo, Executive Director
Purpose: This human rights organization works to conserve indigenous peoples and ethnic minorities in their habitats around the world.
Founded: 1972
FYR: 1990
Revenue: $2,120,707
Expenditures: $2,102,621
1990 membership: 18,000
Staff: 28
Affiliates: Cultural Survival Canada
Topics: Conservation, habitats, indigenous peoples
Approaches: Advocacy, direct action, funding, lobbying, publications, research
Scope: International
Special projects: Rainforest Marketing Project (Brazil)
Periodicals: *The Cultural Survival Quarterly* (magazine)
Books: Yes

Global Tomorrow Coalition
1325 G Street, NW, Suite 915
Washington, DC 20005-3104
Phone: 202-628-4016   Fax: 202-628-4018

Donald R. Lesh, President

Purpose: An umbrella organization uniting 100 NGOs, educational institutions, and corporations in a national network designed to broaden public understanding of long-term global trends in population, resources, environment, and development.

Founded: 1981

FYR: 1990

Revenue: [$496,000]

Expenditures: [$496,000]

1990 membership: 100

Staff: 5

Affiliates: Center for Our Common Future

Topics: All environmental, but especially sustainable development, population

Approaches: Advocacy, conferences, education, grassroots organizing, publications, research

Scope: International

Special projects: United Nations Conference on Environment and Development (Brazil 1992)

Periodicals: *Interaction* (newsletter)

Books: Yes

New Forest Project

International Center for Development Policy

731 8th Street, SE

Washington, DC 20003–2866

Phone: 202-547-3800   Fax: 202-546-4784

Stuart Conway, Director

Purpose: To assist rural villages initiate sustainable development through reforestation projects.

Founded: 1981

FYR: 1988 and 1989

Revenue: $450,691

Expenditures: $420,724

Staff: 3

Topics: Agroforestry, forestry, sustainable development, urban forests

Approaches: Advocacy, education, funding, grassroots organizing, policy, publications, research, technical assistance, training

Scope: Global, with a geographic focus on Latin America, Asia, and the former USSR

Special projects: Guatemala Agroforestry Training Center, Leucaena Seed Project, integrated agriculture/forestry/livestock project in Guatemala, alley cropping program in Belize

Periodicals: *New Forests* (newsletter)

Overseas Development Council

1717 Massachusetts Avenue, NW, Suite 501
Washington, DC 20036
Phone: 202-234-8701   Fax: 202-745-0067
John Sewell, President
Purpose: To analyze economic and political issues of U.S. interdependence with the developing countries of Asia, Africa and Latin America.
Founded: 1971
FYR: 1990
Revenue: $2,252,422
Expenditures: $1,996,064
Staff: 30
Topics: Developing countries, international lending institutions, sustainable development
Approaches: Conferences, publications, research
Scope: International
Special projects: Global Environment Fund, Alternative Budget for New World Order, U.S., Japan, and the Third World

World Development Productions

153A Brattle Street
Cambridge, MA 02138
Phone: 617-497-2323   Fax: 617-497-1616
Richard Harley, Director
Purpose: To produce educational products in print, sound, and video about issues of international development.
Founded: 1988
FYR: 1990
Revenue: Not available

Expenditures: Not available
Staff: 6
Topics: Environment, global change, international debt, sustainable agriculture, sustainable development
Approaches: Education, media, publications
Scope: International
Special projects: PBS television series on hunger and poverty
Books: Yes

❑ *Foundation Funding*

In 1990, about 4 percent of the dollars awarded by U.S. independent and community foundations for environmental programs went for development projects.

❑   ENVIRONMENTAL GRANT-MAKING FOUNDATIONS: ❑
FUNDING FOR DEVELOPMENT PROJECTS 1990

Rank	Foundation	Number of Grants	Dollars Awarded
1	The Rockefeller Foundation	7	2,035,000
2	John D. and Catherine T. MacArthur Foundation	7	1,930,489
3	Rockefeller Brothers Fund	7	618,000
4	The Pew Charitable Trusts	18	579,800
5	The George Gund Foundation	2	529,650
6	Charles Stewart Mott Foundation	8	380,000
7	The Ford Foundation	6	296,000
8	The Tinker Foundation	3	254,000
9	Richard King Mellon Foundation	2	175,000
10	Joyce Mertz-Gilmore Foundation	8	132,500

Index